NETWORKING IS DEAD

NETWORKING IS DEAD

Making Connections That Matter

MELISSA G WILSON AND LARRY MOHL

ROLLING MEADOWS LIBRARY
3110 MARTIN LANE
ROLLING MEADOWS, IL 60008

BENBELLA BOOKS, INC.
DALLAS, TEXAS

This book is a work of fiction. Names, characters, places, and incidents are the product of the author's imagination and are used fictitiously. Any resemblance to actual events, locales or persons, living or dead, is coincidental.

Copyright © 2012 by Melissa G Wilson and Larry Mohl

All rights reserved. No part of this book may be used or reproduced in any manner whatsoever without written permission except in the case of brief quotations embodied in critical articles or reviews.

BenBella Books, Inc.
10300 N. Central Expressway
Suite #400
Dallas, TX 75231
www.benbellabooks.com
Send feedback to feedback@benbellabooks.com

Printed in the United States of America
10 9 8 7 6 5 4 3 2 1

Library of Congress Cataloging-in-Publication Data is available for this title.

978-1-937856-02-1

Editing by Brian Nicol
Copyediting by Deb Kirkby
Proofreading by Cape Cod Compositors, Inc. and Michael Fedison
Indexing by Clive Pyne
Text design and composition by fusion29 and John Reinhardt Book Design
Printed by Berryville Graphics, Inc.

Distributed by Perseus Distribution
perseusdistribution.com

To place orders through Perseus Distribution:
Tel: 800-343-4499
Fax: 800-351-5073
E-mail: orderentry@perseusbooks.com

Significant discounts for bulk sales are available. Please contact Glenn Yeffeth at glenn@benbellabooks.com or 214-750-3628.

I dedicate this book to my great family—
Graham, Gavin, Courtney, David, Katie, and Winnie,
and especially, my husband, Craig, who is my muse!

—MELISSA G WILSON

I dedicate this book to my wife, Carly,
and daughters, Lawson and Erden.
They are my life and my connections
that matter most.

—LARRY MOHL

CONTENTS

NETWORKING IS DEAD

DEFINE YOUR *WHY*

MEREDITH SPOTTED LANCE the minute he walked into the crowded coffee shop. His head was down, his shoulders hunched, fingers clutching the strap of his leather messenger bag tightly. Lance hated crowds.

It was, of course, one of the reasons she'd chosen the Cup of Café in the first place—to ease Lance out of his comfort zone by getting him out of his cloistered corporate office and into the real world.

At 42, Lance looked as dignified as ever in black slacks and purple dress shirt, wearing the lilac tie she'd given him for Christmas. Lance finally spotted her as he took his place in line.

A smile lit up his still-handsome face, then quietly flickered and fizzled out when he saw where she'd placed herself—in a booth smack dab in the middle of the café. She smirked as he wagged a finger; he much preferred a corner booth, out of the busy and noisy coffee shop's hub.

"Why don't we just sit on the counter and put out a tip jar?" Lance grumbled playfully as he sat down across from her, sliding a gingerbread scone across the table in her direction.

She smiled. He knew it was her favorite. "Weren't you the one who wanted to try new things this year? Wasn't 'stretching your boundaries' one of your resolutions?"

Lance fingered the side of his red and green holiday-themed coffee cup. "I suppose," he sighed, taking a sip of his coffee. "I just prefer to do my stretching in private, that's all."

"You can't grow your network in private, Lance," she scolded.

Meredith nibbled on her scone and tried to ignore the bluesy rendition of "Rudolph the Red-Nosed Reindeer" humming away on the café's speakers overhead. "You'd think they'd switch back to normal by now," Lance remarked, as if reading her mind. "I mean, it *is* the fifth of January already."

She chuckled. It had always been like that for Meredith and Lance. Like an old married couple, they could often be found finishing each other's sentences, coming up with the same ideas at the same time, partnering on a variety of side ventures despite their busy professional lives.

Lance had been Meredith's tutor while she majored in business marketing at State, and as their professional relationship grew friendlier, he'd encouraged her to join a few campus clubs to build her list of connections before she graduated.

At 36, Meredith was younger than Lance by more than a few years, but she enjoyed being mentored in various business scenarios as much as she enjoyed mentoring Lance in a variety of social scenarios—Coffee Shop 101, for instance!

How ironic, she mused as they waited for Jill, their mutual friend and yoga instructor, to join them, *that Lance had helped me start my own personal network only to turn into a professional hermit himself!*

"How are the rest of your resolutions going?" Meredith asked, subtly reminding Lance that, after all, this was his big idea for a brighter, more connected new year.

He hoisted his coffee cup to eye level and said, "Well, I'm breaking one as we speak—no more caffeine—and once this meeting with Jill goes bust, that will make two."

"Oh no" Meredith smiled, waving to Jill as she walked through the café door at that precise moment. "It was *your* idea for us both to double our business connections this year, and I'm not going to let either one of us back out of it now."

Meredith watched as Jill flirted lazily with the barista who took her order. She was in her mid-twenties and looked impeccable in fitted linen slacks and a crisp white blouse, but Meredith knew the part-time career coach was far more comfortable in the yoga pants and tank top she wore while putting her and Lance through their paces at her private gym three times a week.

"Happy New Year!" Jill declared cheerfully, joining them at the booth and hugging them both as the scent of her peppermint mocha breezed across the table. "I'm so glad you two reached out to me after the holidays. I have *just* the person to make your New Year's resolution come true."

"You amaze me, Jill," Lance chuckled.

"How's that?" Jill asked, tucking a strand of blond hair behind her ear as she set down her holiday-themed coffee cup.

Lance shrugged. "I just never thought I'd be getting schooled in business networking from the same person who taught me Downward Facing Dog, that's all."

Meredith and Jill chuckled at the same time. "That sounds like a vague insult, Lance," Jill joked, playfully slapping his wrist.

"Not at all," said Lance. "I guess that's the point of making connections, right? You never know when they'll come in handy?"

Jill nodded. "I certainly never opened a gym to make business connections, but when I realized that most of my clients were also lawyers, VPs for Fortune 500 companies, accountants, whatever, it just seemed like a natural outgrowth to start putting them together. That's how I met Dan, who should be here any minute."

"So what's Dan's specialty exactly?" Meredith asked.

Jill reached for a hefty crumb of Meredith's scone and chewed it carefully while forming an answer. "This," she finally said, using her small hands to indicate the collective of three at their booth, and the dozen or more people at the tables on either side of them. "Putting people from diverse backgrounds together."

Meredith was about to ask how he possibly monetized such a skill set, when Jill's hand shot up with a perky wave. Meredith looked toward the door to find a small, rather undistinguished man entering the café.

He behaved much as Lance had, more focused on getting his coffee than on addressing the room. He wore pleated khaki slacks and a generic powder-blue dress shirt, rolled up at the sleeves. He carried no bag, no tablet. From what Meredith could see, he didn't even have a phone on him.

When he finally saw Jill, his face turned warm and inviting with a simple smile of acknowledgement. As he walked to their booth, he made eye contact first with Meredith, then Lance, smiling at them both beneath warm green eyes.

They all stood to greet each other as Jill made the introductions. "Dan," Jill announced brightly as she gestured with open palms toward him. "This is Meredith, founder and CEO of Social Solutions. And this is Lance, head of accounting at Hospitality, Inc. Meredith, Lance, this is, well…this is Dan."

The four of them chuckled anxiously before Jill looked at her watch and said, "Well, that's it for me, gang. My work here is done. Best of luck with the meeting."

"What?" Lance asked, almost pleadingly. "Where are you off to already?"

"My Yoga for Beginners class starts in ten minutes!" she offered, making no more excuses before retreating quickly to her small but intimate yoga studio two blocks away from the Cup of Café.

Admiring Lance's reaction with a bemused grin, Dan said, "I'm surprised she stayed that long or dressed up for that matter. Jill has helped me make introductions in the parking lot behind her gym, at her reception desk, and, once, right outside the men's locker room."

The picture of Jill collaring Dan in his gym clothes clearly put Lance at ease. Dan regarded them both curiously and sipped his cup of coffee. "Jill said you both were resolved to make more connections this year, am I right?"

Meredith nodded. "Yes, Dan, both Lance and I agreed that this year was going to be the 'Year of Networking'!"

Dan reacted to her statement as if he'd just bitten into a lemon seed. "Oooh," he cautioned gently, sucking air through his teeth. "First lesson, let's completely do away with the word 'networking' while we work together. Agreed?"

Lance and Meredith shared a worried look. "But isn't that your specialty, Dan?" Lance asked. "Networking?"

Dan smiled; Meredith liked his smile. "It is, for sure, but networking has gotten such a bad name, especially in this new world of social networking. I prefer to call it what it should be, *making connections that matter*."

Meredith shared another quick glance with Lance. They both nodded, perhaps subconsciously. To her way of thinking, *making connections that matter* sounded a lot more hands on, even more controllable, than *networking*.

Meanwhile, Lance was clearly struggling with the concept. "But isn't networking technically the act of building a network?"

Dan nodded, pulling up his seat a little and growing more animated as he spoke; he clearly relished the subject matter and was interested in helping others achieve his level of success. Meredith silently wondered if that was why he was so good at it.

"It is, certainly," Dan agreed. "But rather than growing a huge network focused on sheer numbers, building a successful network is about establishing a relatively *small number* of *deep, high-quality, business relationships* based on *common values*. Or, as I call it, making connections that matter. In order to do this effectively, you must first clearly define your core values."

Lance's cheeks grew ruddy, a sure sign he was growing more and more agitated. "Small number?" he repeated, also inching forward in his seat a smidge.

He looked at Meredith and chuckled. "But that's why we came to you in the first place, Dan. Or, rather, why we approached Jill. Both Meredith and I already have a *small* network. That's the problem."

"Is it?" Dan countered. "Or is it that you have not created the *right* small network best suited for you to begin with?"

Dan paused to let his words sink in, then continued: "Think about networking for a minute. Think about its evolution. What started out as a great idea, forming relationships and putting friends and allies together in the path of opportunity, has devolved into a common act of collecting as many business cards as possible or in the case of online networking, collecting the most 'friends' and 'followers' as possible. Most people who talk about networking these days are really saying, 'I'm going to mine you for your contacts, use you until you're dry, and then move on.' Am I right?"

Meredith smiled to find Lance nodding enthusiastically. "It has grown rather selfish lately," he agreed.

Dan's eyes grew wider. "Exactly. Selfish, predatory, thoughtless, inauthentic. You go to these networking meetings and it's like speed dating—people come up to you, want to find out what you can do for them, and if you don't fit their narrow picture of what they can get out of you, BOOM!—they're onto the next person."

"So how do we fix that, Dan?" Meredith asked. "I mean, if you're saying networking is broken, how do we fix it?"

"You bring up a good point," Dan answered enthusiastically. "Before we get started *fixing* your networks, I want to know a little bit more about *why* you want to make connections that matter in the first place...I'll start!"

Lance chuckled and Meredith eased into the cushion behind her. She wasn't sure which direction they were headed or even if Dan was the proper guide for their journey, but she'd made a New Year's resolution to grow her network—sorry, make more meaningful connections—and if he could help, even a little, it was worth a cup of coffee and a few minutes of her time.

She could tell by Lance's more relaxed posture and expression of anticipation that he was feeling the same way.

Dan paused for a few moments before saying, "I was a teacher for many years. I was good at it, but I was better at helping people, one-on-one, improve their lives. That's why I went into teaching: to improve the lives of kids who might not be as fortunate as I was growing up. But it was stifling, working within the politics of the other teachers, under such careful scrutiny by the school board and the administration. Frankly, I was much more successful at putting the kids' parents in touch with a great tutor or the right guidance counselor than I ever was teaching math or science!"

Still unsure where Dan was headed, Meredith smiled encouragingly; she was eager to hear more.

"So one summer, while I was still getting paid for the teaching work I'd done that year but didn't have to go into the classroom anymore, I started a small company called Tutor Tech. It was basically me in my den with a computer, a phone, and a fax putting kids together with local tutors. Their parents paid me a small finder's fee. It was fun and I had more freedom than in the classroom.

"By mid-July, I knew I'd never go back to school. Fortunately, one of the kids' parents worked at a top recruiting firm for C-level players. He saw what I was doing for his kid and figured I could do it for him. So he hired me, full-time, to recruit. That was the first time I ever realized the power of making connections that matter. I used that power at his recruiting firm, but after a few years it was like teaching all over again—four walls and too much politics.

"It paid well though, and after living on a teacher's salary for so long, I kept my frugal habits. At the recruiting firm, my deals brought me double-digit commissions and bonuses, and I managed to save up quite a bit. I used my solid savings to go back into my own company, but this time I didn't limit myself. I started Connections Count in the same office I use today, but I barely use it. I'm too busy making, well, connections that count."

Meredith nodded; her story sounded very similar to Dan's. As if sensing this, he said, "But you're not here to listen to me talk about myself. Now I want to know a little bit more about you two. Meredith, what do you do at Social Solutions?"

"It's a social media consulting and implementation firm," Meredith said, quickly falling into the rhythm of her elevator pitch. "I talk to a client about his or her needs and then draw up a personalized plan for customizing their Facebook page, learning how to engage on Twitter and keep their content streaming, deciding which LinkedIn profiles in their company need makeovers, and building an online presence, all in a time-effective manner."

Dan smiled. "So it sounds very specialized and hands on."

Meredith brightened. "It is! I spend about a week with each client, working their schedules, touring the facility, if there is one, really getting to know them and their products inside and out. It's the only way to do what I do effectively, and it really gives me insight on how to help them. I think that's why I get so much repeat business."

Dan smirked. "Repeat business but not *new* business, am I right?"

She nodded reluctantly. "I network like crazy. Sorry, I know you hate that word, but...nothing new seems to come in. I can't figure out what I'm doing wrong."

Dan reassured her. "I wouldn't say you're doing anything wrong. It's just that repeat business is a little like swimming in the same fishbowl. After a while, you've got nowhere else to go. And people are protective, self-protective. They want you all to themselves, ready at a moment's notice to fix their problems, so it's not really in their best interest to give you a ton of new business with their friends and family."

Dan spoke to what Meredith had long suspected; she nodded in reply.

"And, Lance," he asked, shifting gears or at least perspectives. "How about you? What's Hospitality, Inc., all about?"

Lance cleared his throat and gave his elevator speech: "We're an accounting firm that specializes in the hospitality business—restaurants mostly."

Dan looked impressed. "So you've both been successful finding your niche and becoming successful there. But now it sounds like you've plateaued. Is that about right?"

Meredith and Lance both nodded.

"And Lance, Meredith explained a little why she's here; how about you?"

Lance shrugged. "It's like you said, Dan; I've reached a plateau. I'm successful at work, but I could be doing so much more for my clients, for myself. Accounting is more than just numbers; it's about making the best use of your assets. Or at least it can be if done right. I see so many restaurants close down or go bankrupt, not because they weren't successful but because they couldn't manage their money. I want to help more of them avoid that, but I can't if I don't reach out to more."

Dan was nodding vigorously. "I think we're getting somewhere. You both have very strong reasons for making connections that matter. It just sounds like you haven't been doing it the right way. So, Meredith, help me help you: What is your definition of networking?"

Uncertain, Meredith glanced at Lance, who smirked back at her with an expression that said, *Better you than me.*

She cleared her throat and said, "Well, I attend a lot of networking events. Our local chamber of commerce has a popular 'Wednesday Friends Day' event that I go to each month, and I generally make it a habit to come away with at least a dozen new introductions. Then I follow up those leads before the next month's Friends Day event."

Dan clearly looked dubious. "And how is that working out for you?"

Meredith found herself chuckling. "Well," she said in reply, "I'm here, aren't I?"

"And Lance, how about you?"

Lance looked uncomfortable. "I attended one of those events with Meredith, but...they just weren't for me. So recently I've been trying to schedule more meetings with clients. Generally I can do their accounting via phone, fax, e-mail, and the like, but I've been diligent about getting out into their natural habitat and hoping to make some connections there."

Lance paused, then sat back, indicating he was finished. Now that she'd heard their pitiful attempts at networking spoken aloud, Meredith felt even worse than before.

But Dan brightened and said, "The good news is that you guys have all the tools to build *great* connections that matter. The bad news is, I think you have your *what* confused with your *why*."

Seeing the questioning looks on their faces, Dan continued, "If you ask most people *what* they are trying accomplish or *how* they intend to accomplish it, it's something they can usually easily tell you. For instance, Lance, if I'd asked you, 'What do you want to accomplish in the new year?' chances are you'd still be talking as they closed this place down later tonight."

All three of them laughed and Meredith could almost see Lance's resistance crumble in the face of Dan's power of reasoning. "And you, Meredith," Dan continued, casting his green eyes in her direction. "If I'd asked you *how* you were going to add more connections to your present list, you could have talked me through three more cups of coffee.

"But if you ask people *why* they are doing what they are doing, their answers become far less clear. In fact, most people have *why* and *what* confused. 'I need to network in order to find a piece of business or create a new gadget' are certainly very real and practical concerns. However, if you 'double-click' on your *why*, asking a deeper *why*, new questions and opportunities appear. When your reason *why* is bigger than your *what* or your *how*, you become an *attractor of possibility*. What's more, you inspire connections and more opportunities.

"For example, Meredith, you might state, 'I am working in social media consulting because I want to help people grow their businesses more successfully and because I have seen that the Web can offer them so much more opportunity at a lower cost. I am therefore passionate about helping others get online.' Or, for you, Lance, you might say, 'I am working at this accounting firm because they focus on restaurants and I love helping restaurants become more successful.' With these reasons you become magnets for connection because you know *why* you want to make connections that matter."

Dan paused to catch his breath; his face was flushed with excitement and, Meredith had to admit, it was catching. She had never paused to consider the *why* of networking and told him so.

"I guess the *why* just always seemed obvious to me," she admitted, almost sheepishly. "I just assumed others would somehow know my *why* for doing what I do."

Lance and Dan were both nodding furiously but, it would appear, for different reasons.

"That's the problem, Meredith," said Dan. "We assume we know the obvious *why* for monetizing the process, but in fact that's not a good enough question. We need to dig deeper if we want to be truly successful at growing our best business relationships, at making connections that matter."

Lance looked from Meredith to Dan and asked, "Forgive my ignorance but...why?"

Meredith found herself nodding in commiseration. Assume or not, Meredith was pretty sure she already knew why she was meeting with Dan. Then again, she could always be wrong.

"Good question, Lance, and not ignorant at all. Just the opposite, in fact. Exploring these questions provides clarity of purpose and sets you up to build your network with purpose and persistence, because a more deeply held purpose is essential for sticking with things as you encounter the inevitable bumps in the road. The *why* of connecting is also focused on people first, opportunities second.

"If you take this first big step, you will act in an authentic and credible way as you go about your community building or, as you call it, 'networking.' Those who build successful networks start by spending at least 30 minutes weekly reflecting on their values and purpose, refining them, and assessing them to see if their actions, values, and purpose are in alignment. It's about slowing down to speed up actually."

"Thirty minutes?" Meredith interrupted skeptically. She could barely spare that much time for something critical like a business meeting or afternoon workout. For network building? She was growing more skeptical by the minute. "Why so much time?"

Dan smirked and said, "What, you want the cow and the milk on the same day?"

All three laughed. "Trust me, if we can meet, say, once a week you will know how to do this by the end of January. And that weekly 30-minute investment will be the best you've ever made. What's more, it will become a habit for the rest of your life."

Meredith and Lance shrugged. Lance said, "What next?"

"In addition to the *why* behind your need for more connections, we need to drill down to your vision. Your vision is a picture of your ideal future and acts as a powerful magnet to draw you closer to your future. Some visions are very specific, like what their office building will look like, while others are more general, outlining future direction and attributes. Either is okay."

Dan paused and Meredith took advantage of it to ask, "Do you mind, Dan, sharing with us your vision?"

Dan nodded. "My vision is to help others succeed through my unique experience with building connections that matter, which directly ties into my *why*.

"Over time and through this process, you continue to clarify and specify a future vision that expresses your purpose and values in your work and life. You should spend time weekly reflecting on your vision, refining it, and assessing if your actions align with it. Again, those people who have inspiring visions pull others along on their journey.

"The most important thing is to have a *why* that emanates from a deep passion. And that the passion must be focused and have a core around making a difference for others—not just yourself. For example, look at Steve Jobs. He had a big passion in life—to make a beautifully engineered computer. He honed his passion and pushed to get his product out to as many people as possible. He wanted to make a difference in how people experienced technology. His *why* changed the world."

Meredith found herself nodding and, surprised by the silence in the wake of Dan's explanation, looked up to find the mid-afternoon crowd mostly gone.

Now she stared out at a half-empty café, still festooned with the corporate signage wishing guests "Happy Holidays" and a blinking tree by the condiment stand.

A slightly jazzy riff on "White Christmas" played overhead as she asked, "So, Dan, now that you've completely revolutionized how we think about making connections that matter, what should we focus on next?"

"I'm glad you asked." Dan smirked, sliding his empty coffee cup away from him. "For your homework, I'd like you to define your *why*, core values, and vision in two paragraphs and/or pictures and bring them to the next meeting."

Meredith made a note on her iPhone as Lance scribbled the instructions on the back of a Cup of Café napkin. Dan then stood and said a quick good-bye. As he headed out the doorway, he turned to them and added, "And bring your list of contacts. Here is a cheat sheet, if you will, to help. I always find that putting things in writing adds to whatever you share verbally."

Dan gave the two of them one last big smile as he set down two sheets of paper with type on just one side.

Meredith and Lance looked over their respective guides, nodding their heads almost in unison. The guides simply stated:

. . . .

DAN'S FIRST-LESSON TIPS

✓ Shift from traditional networking to making connections that matter.

✓ This is how you create better and more sustainable connections.

✓ Figure out what matters to you most in the work you do currently or the work you would like to do.

✓ Add to your list of what core values matter most—values such as security or freedom (many entrepreneurs choose this value), creativity, integrity, etc.

✓ Next, write down and/or find images that fit your vision of what your life will look like when what matters most to you is combined with a great network of like-valued connections, and you have achieved what you define as success.

✓ When you share what matters to you explicitly, rather than just assuming people will know what matters to you, you start building a great network and become an attractor of possibility.

CREATE QUALITY OVER QUANTITY

L ANCE WAS NOT generally a procrastinator. He couldn't afford to be. His job required him to think and act quickly, to notice the details and troubleshoot the problems before they began, not after they had blossomed into full-blown crises for his clients in the hospitality industry.

But he was finding Dan's homework more off-putting than he'd first anticipated. The lesson, he knew, was simple: all he needed to do was write two paragraphs defining his *why*, his *core values*, and his *vision*. Not a big deal. It was the same kind of exercise he did at Hospitality, Inc., corporate retreats every other year or so.

But this was personal. His personal network, or whatever Dan wanted them to call it, was his Achilles' heel. It was too small, Lance felt, too isolated, too internal, not dynamic, helpful, or generous enough. Not so much for Meredith, who was as outgoing, friendly, and popular as an adult could be!

He grumbled and bent down to hit the Word icon on his computer, opening a blank document and titling it simply, "Dan's Homework Assignment #1."

It felt good to be moving on something, to hear the click of the keyboard beneath his fingers and the black words filling the white page. With time running out before their next meeting, Lance decided just to grin and bear it—so he could get it over with. If he did it wrong, or misunderstood the question, he figured Dan would set him straight at their meeting.

It wasn't like he was getting graded on this stuff, right?

"Why do I want to increase my social network?" He began typing. "Because it's too small. It doesn't offer me the right opportunities and if I'm ever going to get anywhere in my professional life, I need more opportunities, not less.

"This ties directly into my core values, which include solving complex problems for, and with, like-minded people. Nothing satisfies me more than coming to a problem cold, finding a solution, and making someone's day. Finally, my vision for building a values-based network is to connect with like-valued people for our individual and mutual benefit."

Lance finished typing, hit "Save," and reread his work. He smiled but only weakly. He was done, even if the assignment sounded more like he was filling out a resume or job application than approaching a new endeavor. He wished Meredith would have taken him up on his offer to work together on this, but she'd insisted that they both do their homework alone.

Lance looked at his watch and realized he only had a few minutes to print his homework and scoot if he wanted to make his afternoon meeting with Dan and Meredith across town.

· · · · · ·

The conference room was small but uncluttered— rather than using rows and rows of seats, it was set up with three small working areas, each with a comfortable leather chair and small coffee table in front.

"Is it always set up like this?" Lance asked curiously, nodding to Meredith and Dan, who were milling about the middle of the room. "I mean, this is pretty valuable space for a hotel."

Dan winked and said, "Let's just say I make it worth their while to provide me with a comfortable sitting area. Will this do, Lance?"

"It's great," Lance proclaimed. "It's just, when you said we'd be meeting at the Morecraft Hotel, I was picturing one of those drab conference rooms with the podium and rows of chairs."

Dan chuckled. "Oh, they have those, too, but I decided to make mine a little more comfortable."

"That it is," Lance said, admiring the cozy touches for their meeting. A wide array of sodas, cookies, chips, and ice lined a small buffet table, stacked with cups and napkins for their convenience. "It's like a mini-workshop."

"That's how I like to see it," Dan said, sitting down in his own seat to signal the meeting could begin. "I tend to come here a lot. My office isn't really set up for meetings, and when we meet at a client's office, it becomes more like work. This way, you're more open to interpretation."

Lance smiled at Meredith, who looked as nervous as he felt. "Will we be meeting here every week, Dan?" she asked.

He nodded. "It's my office away from my office. I hope you don't mind."

Lance sat and fingered his homework nervously.

Dan gave him a sympathetic look and said, "Lance, you look a little anxious about last week's assignment. How about we take a look at yours first and put your mind at ease?"

Lance chuckled to be figured out so easily. "If you insist." He groaned playfully, handing over his assignment.

Dan looked at it and, for Meredith's benefit, read it aloud. Lance watched his old friend's face as she heard his why, core values, and vision read to her; she was nodding by the end.

When Dan was finished reading, he put the sheet of paper down in front of him and looked back at Lance. "That's a great start," he said encouragingly before turning to Meredith. "Your turn."

Meredith looked down sheepishly at the leather laptop bag at her feet. "If you insist," she said, sliding out an 8×10 photo and handing it to Dan. When he raised his eyes quizzically, she said, "You told us we could bring a picture!"

He smiled, offering a wry chuckle. "I suppose I did, Meredith. It's just, no one's ever done so before."

Dan studied the picture carefully for a moment, smiled, and then turned it around so that Lance and Meredith could see. Lance smiled; it was a piece of stock photography he had helped her pick when she designed her first brochure years earlier.

It showed a small group of people, men and women, black and white, Asian and Hispanic, all in business suits gathered at a conference table. They were smiling and joking but clearly working on a big project together. Outside the windows of the office building the sky was dark; the three men pictured in the center had their sleeves rolled up, their ties loosened. It looked like the whole group was in for a long night of working together.

"Meredith?" Dan asked, looking sideways at the smiling office workers pictured. "Care to walk us through this?"

"Sure," she said. "I thought this picture perfectly represented my *why* for identifying my connections that matter versus just unconsciously adding people—so-called friends I don't know well or at all—in hopes that such a strategy will help me increase my success in my business.

"As you shared last week, I should collaborate with a few well-targeted people just like these who can help find more people just like themselves. In other words, these quality connections will lead to new and more quality connections. This picture also perfectly represents my core values, which are helping people help themselves. Finally, this is my own personal vision of success: a group of like-minded people working together to solve a problem."

Meredith sat back in her chair, satisfied. Lance gave her a little *good job* nod and she smiled in recognition. Dan nodded and slid Meredith's picture on top of Lance's homework.

Then he sat back, crossed his legs, and laced his fingers under his chin. "Both of you," he began cautiously, "before I begin, I want to say you're both off to a great start. I really like the creativity and enthusiasm you expended on this homework assignment I gave you last week and it's clear you put a lot of thought into it. But I think you've still got your *why* and your *what* mixed up. Let me back up and double-click on that for you so we're clear before moving ahead . . ."

Dan paused, sitting up a bit, then continued: "I think the word that's missing from your *why* answers is *because*. What I heard from you, Lance, was what you want to do—grow a network, work with like-minded people, etc. And you, Meredith, same thing—what you want to do is collaborate with like-minded people, work on solving their problems and finding solutions, etc. Those are all worthy answers, but what I'm still not hearing is the *why* because you didn't give me a *because*. I am looking for the *deeper why* beyond the surface reasons you have shared. What lies in your core that drives you to want to accomplish your goals?"

"You mean more like 'cause and effect,' Dan?" Meredith asked.

Dan nodded. "Yes, Meredith. What you guys are giving me is more of a surface answer. Dig deeper into the specific reason as to *why* you need or want other people to help you solve problems, Lance, or *why* being in a group is so appealing to you, Meredith."

Lance nodded. That made sense. Dan continued, "Remember during our first meeting, one of the *why* examples I used was this one for you, Lance. 'I am working at this accounting firm because they focus on restaurants and I love helping restaurants become more successful.'"

Lance was impressed. "You remembered it verbatim?"

Dan chuckled. "I liked it a lot, Lance, and here's why: all of us have this reason within a reason for what we do. Why am I here talking to you two today? Because I love sharing this information with folks who have so much potential really to explode these ideas off of paper and into real life. That's my *why*. Now we need to find your reason within a reason—your *why*. Lance, let's start with you. Finish this sentence: I work at an accounting firm that specializes in restaurants because..."

Lance hemmed before suddenly growing inspired: "I work at an accounting firm that specializes in restaurants because...I want to help them be successful."

"That's great, Lance," acknowledged Dan with an enthusiastic nod. "But we can go one step further. Consider this as your *why* statement, Lance: I want them to be successful because I believe restaurants are a place where people come together to share their lives and build relationships. Additionally, I like working with family-owned restaurants because they have so much more invested in their businesses. Many of these family-owned restaurants get passed down from one generation to the next. The passion these families have for their business is intoxicating. They make me feel part of their family."

Lance smiled in pleasant surprise at Dan's attempt to articulate in words how Lance felt deep down. He nodded and so did Meredith. "I've seen Lance at work, Dan," she said, "and he really does come to life when he's walking around the kitchen, especially with a mom-and-pop restaurant where he gets to show them the different ways they can save or maximize their money."

Lance felt this was true.

"Now we are starting to get to the heart of the matter for Lance," Dan explained. "His underlying *why* for connecting with more people is to help build generations of family-owned businesses, and in doing this, he is helping people build wonderful, prosperous, joyful lives. Now he has further defined *why* he wants to build a better network."

Lance was nodding and blurted, "These families move from a position of working to live to living to work in a great, innovative environment. I then become a maestro or facilitator, helping these families become the leaders in their markets!"

"Nice!" Dan said. "Now we're getting to the heart of why you're here, and now you can better understand your motivations for coming to me in the first place. You can also open yourself up to meeting the right types of people by probing deeper into why you do what you do and your vision that ties into your passion. This statement goes one step deeper into what is personally important to you and sets the context for making meaningful connections for you. It also reveals your unique differentiator that attracts more of those perfect clients you want in your network."

Dan turned to Meredith. "Your turn, Meredith. Finish this sentence for me: I am eager to grow my list of meaningful connections because . . ."

Meredith was ready, quickly answering, "Because I already work so well with others in my firm. I know that there are many talented, young, social media sensations interning at my firm and I want to learn from them because I know they have so much to offer. In return, I get the chance to mentor the next generation of public relations stars and that is exciting—and rewarding!"

Dan was nodding halfway through her explanation, letting them both know that Meredith was on the right track as well.

"Okay, Meredith, great, but let's dig a little deeper. Keep it succinct and simple, like Lance's."

Meredith thought and Lance could see the smile on her face when the lightbulb came on: "I provide custom social media solutions to small business by building intimate relationships..."

Dan smirked. "That's a great descriptor for your business card, Meredith, but let's not forget the *why* inherent in your answer. In other words, you left out the *because* from your response."

Meredith looked chagrined as she replied, "I am eager to grow my list of meaningful connections because...it is a great feeling to help others express their business in an authentic way."

This time Dan leaned forward, clapping his hands. "And?" he prompted, eager to have Meredith dig as deeply as Lance had to find her *reason within a reason*.

Thus inspired, Meredith added, "Because...I believe that much of social media is just spin, and when you help someone tell their authentic story, you are truly contributing to their success professionally and personally. And with the new young talent I have turned into a collaborative team, I combine my seasoned wisdom with their insatiable passion and ability to leverage the most cutting-edge technologies. It's a huge win-win!"

Dan's smile of satisfaction and the ease of his posture as he sat back into his seat was validation enough that Meredith was now digging deeper as well.

"This is great progress, gang," Dan said. "Your *why* isn't just about your motivation. It's about discovering a deeper, guiding purpose and a stronger set of values. Now, let's compare your visions. Lance, you first said, and I quote, 'My vision for building a successful network is to connect with like-minded people with mutual interests for our mutual benefit.' Am I right, Lance?"

Lance nodded, but now in the light of what Dan had just shared, that didn't sound like a vision at all.

"And, Meredith?" Dan continued. "I didn't memorize your vision so why don't you remind me of it again?"

Meredith looked uncertainly over at Lance. "I dunno," she confessed. "I'm not so sure mine is accurate anymore."

Dan smiled, nodding. "That's okay, Meredith. Whatever it is, there is truth to it and we'll refine it over time. After all, this is a process."

Dan's words made Lance feel better. Meredith nodded and said, "Well, I explained earlier that my vision is to 'join a group of like-minded people working together to solve a problem.'"

Dan let Meredith's vision sit there for a few moments. She quickly added, "But that doesn't sound very specific anymore, does it?"

Dan shook his head. "Actually, it's fairly specific in the sense that it aligns closely with your *why*. Lance, however, yours is a little vague; it sounds more like a homework answer than real soul searching. But that's okay. We're going to work together to refine these until you really hone your vision."

Lance nodded. "But what can we do, between these meetings, to help refine our visions?"

Meredith winked. "I think I know. This is where those 30 minutes a week come in, right, Dan?"

"That's right, Meredith. I want you to just find a quiet space, removed from your usual work space, and spend at least 30 minutes once a week reflecting on your vision, refining it, and assessing if your actions and more importantly, your connections, align with it. It's very important that you refine your visions throughout this process so that you build your network successfully, benefiting you, your connections, and the ripples of connections that are forever impacted because of wiser choices."

Dan sat back, crossed his legs, and picked a piece of lint off one shirtsleeve. "But that's more homework. For now, I want to get to the point of this week's lesson, which is to choose 'quality partners' for your network."

He then stood and approached a whiteboard affixed to the hotel conference room wall, and grabbed some markers from the attached tray. With a red marker, he drew a small circle in the middle of the board, then with a green marker, he drew a slightly larger circle around the first. Inside the first circle, he drew a "10" and outside the second, a "20." Finally, he used a blue marker to draw a much bigger circle around both the red and green circles and wrote "All the Rest" inside it.

When he was done, he put the green marker down and used the red one as a kind of pointer. He paced slowly, his dark brown loafers whispering softly on the thin conference room carpet.

"What you see on the board is what I want you to focus on this week. Here in the smaller circle, I want you to seek 10 or fewer people for this first circle. I call this your 'Primary Circle.' This second outside circle in green I call your 'Secondary Circle.' Here, I want you to seek no more than an additional 20 people."

Lance nodded cautiously, tossing a look to Meredith, who seemed equally pensive. Dan continued: "Every well-functioning network has an inner circle—a Primary Circle—and a Secondary Circle and a Tertiary Circle. Identifying these three sets of circles helps you organize your relationships and focus your energy on the right people at the right time. Your Primary Circle is critical. Within your Primary Circle should be those people who most closely align with your values and goals. These are those 'partners' with whom you will have the most frequent contact and support exchanges.

"This circle should hold no more than 10 influential people. Your outer circles represent weaker ties, but those people are still valuable. Those within your outer circles are usually great sources of information, referrals, and ideas. It's impossible to have strong bonds with too many people at one time—it becomes impossible to connect deeply with more than 15 people on a regular basis. For business purposes, I have found it is easiest to focus on just 10 people."

Lance listened with growing alarm. So far Dan had made sense—the why, the what, the how, even the vision. It was all going in the right direction. But this? This? He hadn't signed up to get together every week simply to meet just 20 or 30 new people. He needed a network, not a knitting group!

"Lance?" Dan asked cautiously, an understanding smile formed on his face as he reached over to the buffet table and cracked open a can of diet soda. "You look perplexed. Care to share?"

"I just, w-w-well," he stammered, "I can't do anything with that amount of people."

"Me either," snapped Meredith, standing up to pour herself a cup of coffee, but Lance knew there was more to it than that. She liked to pace when she was upset. "I mean, I could fill three or more circles as we speak."

Dan smiled, sipping at his soda before responding, "Yes, but...would they be quality people? Would they be connections or distractions? Friends or...filler?"

"How do you mean?" asked Lance.

"As a colleague of mine has stated, 'You're the sum total of the 10 people you spend the most time with.' Think about it," Dan explained. "Each of us in this room has hundreds if not thousands of connections—'friends' on Facebook, on Twitter, on LinkedIn and Google Plus and Pinterest, through various professional organizations we belong to, lists and blogs we subscribe to, the business cards we've collected, even old college roommates and colleagues, but...how often do we interact with them? Daily? Or more like weekly? Monthly? Or annually? In a world where social capital has value in the billions of dollars, our individual social capital needs to be recognized, developed, and sustained."

Dan paused, then took their silence as a reply. "These *thousands* of connections are not the ones we network with daily or even regularly because it would be physically impossible to do so. Instead, by focusing on a few quality connections to exchange with regularly, you will actually achieve better results faster."

"How can I achieve better results with so few people, Dan?" Meredith asked, giving voice to the same thought Lance was having. "I'm ready, I'm invested in this. I can reach two, three times that many people per day. I mean, I'm willing to invest an hour or more per day in connecting here! Isn't it all about filling that pipeline so that we reach our quotas?"

"But why?" Dan asked. "Why spend an hour or more making short-term, even fleeting connections with more people when you could spend less time having more impact on just one or two people per week? If they are the right people, then you will get to your goals faster. These people would have influence. They would connect you to others. They, like you will be doing, have started with a small *quality* group of connections to build to a *quantity* of *quality* connections!"

"But what would that look like?" Lance asked.

Dan nodded in reply. "Okay, Meredith, let's start with you. If you were to choose just 10 names to put in this first circle, who would be your first five—people you currently know—to go in here?"

Dan uncapped a black marker and waited anxiously, reminding her, "I'm not going to expand the circle, so be careful. Don't pick the biggest, most important names in your network, but those you can realistically interact with this coming week and who might benefit the most from your collaboration."

Lance found himself joining Meredith and Dan at the dry erase board, even as Meredith panicked. "Well, let's start with Lee. He runs the print shop over on Croft Street, and he expressed an interest in partnering on some marketing initiatives. But I don't know about Sylvia. She said she wanted to connect about a new business venture, but she keeps putting me off…"

It went like that, back and forth, for the next half hour. Lance was glad it was a dry erase board or Dan's hands might be permanently stained.

"It's harder than it looks, isn't it?" Dan finally chuckled, putting the cap back on his pen and taking his soda back to his seat.

They joined him, nibbling on snacks and sipping coffee.

The exercise was a valuable one but left Lance feeling less than energized. Although Meredith was stymied simply because she had so many contacts, Lance had the opposite problem: he had too few!

He was struggling trying to identify five people to put in his Primary Circle, let alone 20 to fill his expanded Secondary Circle.

As usual, Dan's green eyes homed in on his insecurity. "Lance, a problem with this week's homework?"

Lance confessed, "I just don't know that many people, Dan. That's why I came to you."

Dan nodded and said, "Actually, Lance, you're in a slightly better position than Meredith on this one."

Meredith bit. "Say what?" she chuckled. Lance did, too. After all, she was always on him to network more, meet more people, and take more chances. Meeting with Dan had been her idea from the start.

Dan held his hands up in mock defeat. "I'm saying, Lance can start from scratch, Meredith, where you'll have to kind of 'unlearn' the way you've been taught to network. For instance, whereas you're having trouble whittling down your connections to fit in your Primary Circle, Lance can choose his from the ground up. He can choose them more wisely, perhaps, going for *local* rather than *long-distance* connections and going for *less* versus *more*. It's really a mindset, this quality over quantity concentration. And unfortunately, Meredith, it's easier to learn a new habit than unlearn a bad one."

As Meredith nodded thoughtfully, no doubt wondering how her instincts for quality over quantity could have been so wrong, Lance saw an opening. "Now can you connect us to some quality people you know?"

Dan didn't answer. He smiled instead. "We'll get to that, guys, but for now I want you to go through your contact lists and actively look for people who share the values you stated for me today, and those with whom you think you could develop a better relationship. These should also be people you *believe* would have strong, vibrant networks."

Meredith nodded, making a note on her iPhone. Lance knew she'd find this part of their homework easy. After all, she had more than 150 contacts and could easily find someone to complement her values and vision. Lance knew it would be a much bigger struggle for himself. After all, his list of contacts had only eight people on it—mostly people from his church or neighborhood, all of whom he knew quite well—but he didn't think they had big networks. The rest were people in his office, such as his project team, but strangely he had never talked much about the quality of their networks within the last couple of years. They had been too busy working on projects that came their way. Neither he nor his other partners realized until recently that the opportunities that *used* to come to them monthly were now coming much less frequently. They were suffering from the downturn big-time!

Taking pity on Lance, Dan looked at him and said, "I'll get you started. First, list two people in your company who you admire but don't know very well."

Lance nodded, then asked, "What if I admire them and know them, what then?"

"We'll get to those later. First, you know how sometimes in school your teacher would partner you with someone new, just to get you out of the rut of sitting with the same people all the time?"

When Meredith and Lance both nodded, Dan continued, "This is a little bit like that. Part of my process involves taking a fresh look at your existing contacts and selectively deepening them. If you are in a larger organization, most of the people in your Primary Circle will be people in your company—at least in the beginning."

Dan smiled, looking at his watch and noting that their time together was drawing to a close. He started gathering up his things. Meanwhile, Lance felt a wave of dread wash over him. He hadn't been looking forward to these weekly meetings, but now that their first one was nearly over, he wished he could spend twice as long learning from Dan!

"The question to ask," Dan continued, "is what percentage of your current network is made up of *Givers, Takers,* and *Exchangers.* You might think Givers are the ideal connections, but in fact, your goal is to find those who are or can become Exchangers."

"What's the difference?" Lance asked. "Don't Givers exchange and Exchangers give?"

He looked to Meredith, who was nodding in agreement. They both looked back to Dan, who replied, "Not exactly. Exchangers are definitely Givers, but they are also good at making requests for support and then *exchanging* opportunities that create a more sustainable model for ongoing, *mutual* success. Exchangers are also good at *discerning* who would be other great connections—other Exchangers to whom to introduce you, to help you grow your network." Dan paused for a moment to let this statement sink in. Meredith and Lance were unusually quiet, their heads nodding, their eyes twinkling in anticipation.

"So this week, your goal is to figure out who are Takers, Givers, and Exchangers—up to 10 people who you already know and five you don't know. The latter five will be people you can be introduced to through those you know. Given that you don't know these additional five yet, write down ideas as to what professions they are in or on what levels they are in an organization.

A lot of people don't understand that you can get to those great, *additional* five through people you currently know. The process is about first finding Givers who might be potential Exchangers."

Meredith nodded, furiously taking notes, then looked up. "Can you go into a little more detail about Exchangers, Dan?"

He smiled, stood, and walked back to the dry erase board. Without another word, he wrote *Exchangers* on the board, then continued writing until he had composed this bullet list:

- Demonstrate a concern for your issues and needs.
- Work to create an equal exchange of information and leads.
- Make an effort to stay in touch with you.
- Provide assistance without talking about how much they're doing for you or without keeping score.

Lance finished taking notes as Dan turned around. He had a smile and a parting message for them. "Listen, I know this is counter to all you've learned before about networking—more is more, bigger is better. Frankly, I blame the Internet."

Both Lance and Meredith looked at him quizzically.

"Online, many people get confused because the world of social networking and social media call connections 'friends.' Even more confusing is the concept of Six Degrees of Separation. Now, sites like LinkedIn let people see who you know (your first-degree connections), who those people know (your second-degree connections), and even who *those* people know (your third-degree connections).

"Remember we talked about your Circles? Well, LinkedIn is a great example of this concept playing out in your daily work life.

"This new vista of connections can overwhelm even the heartiest of *networkers* as they see that their 5,000 first-degree connections can connect them to 3 million second-degree connections and more than 15 million third-degree connections and those second- and third-degree numbers increase daily. What was once your small network of friends and family is now a world of connections and possibilities. But it is also often overwhelming and daunting to keep up with these numbers. How do you pick the quality out of the quantity of connections you have or could be making? How can you not confuse *activity* with *accomplishment*?

"Only by focusing on a few, high-quality connections—10 or fewer at first—can you truly accelerate your goal achievement. It's paradoxical, but starting *small* to grow a *big* network is the way to go. But who are the right, quality connections people to choose to start growing first? Who is your Primary Circle?

"The answer is to *start with those you know* and ask whether each is a Giver, Taker, or Exchanger. Part of being successful with this first step is taking a fresh look at your existing connections and selectively deepening them. As I said before, if you are in a large organization, most of the people in your Primary Circle should be people in your company."

The learning duo spent the next several minutes going through their assignment and, once again, they each got a one-page list of tips from Dan. Dan left them in deep concentration looking over their notes and their tips sheets. He knew they would have their work cut out for them.

DAN'S SECOND-LESSON TIPS

✓ Quality trumps quantity when it comes to building a successful network.

✓ Because the most beneficial opportunities come from people best suited for you, it pays to take time to find the right people, who will have similar and complementary values to network with one-on-one.

✓ From your quality connections come more opportunities. The idea is to go deep first in order to go wide later, instead of going an inch deep with everyone in the world.

✓ Figure out the percentage of Givers, Takers, and Exchangers in your network.

✓ You will most likely find that you will be starting with more Takers than Givers or Exchangers, but be persistent. Your first step will likely be finding Givers who are interested in building "exchanging" opportunities for one another. Those people exist!

✓ It's not easy to trim a high-quantity network into a high-quality network, but it will be rewarding if you invest your time in doing so.

LESSON 3

DIG BELOW THE SURFACE

"YOU DIDN'T HAVE TO do that," Meredith exclaimed a few days later as her 2:30 P.M. appointment, Ariel Cruz, sauntered into the office, gift basket in hand.

But you've done so much for my greeting card company," Ariel insisted, shoving the basket closer toward Meredith on her cluttered desk.

Meredith stood and the two embraced. "That's what you pay me for," Meredith tsk-tsked, then widened her eyes at the wide array of fresh fruit and baked goodies that filled the basket.

"Have you ever thought of going into the bakery business?" Meredith asked as she joined Ariel in the seating cluster on the other side of her desk.

Ariel smiled wickedly and said, "As a matter of fact, Meredith, that's why I'm here today. Not the bakery business, but I am thinking of doing a major geographic expansion and I wanted to bounce some ideas off you."

A couple of hours later, Meredith was just recovering from her whirlwind meeting with Ariel when Chuck, her four-thirty appointment, came in. Chuck was a long-standing client who ran a local landscaping empire—an empire, Meredith realized, she'd been instrumental in building.

"Hey, Meredith," Chuck said, taking off his sunglasses and sitting down. She'd barely had time to stand up to greet him, so she stayed behind her desk.

"How is everything, Chuck? I know you said today's meeting was urgent."

Meredith tried to keep the sarcasm out of her tone. With Chuck, every meeting was urgent.

"Well, it's about the new Web site. I've still got some issues with the layout, and I was hoping I could walk you through them."

Meredith gritted her teeth and pulled up his site on the widescreen monitor affixed to her wall. She used her laser pen as the pointer as Chuck aired his latest complaints.

While they discussed color schemes and more design options, Meredith realized that this was his fifth set of revisions so far, with no end in sight. What's more, he was still an invoice or two behind, and he had yet to introduce her to that client of his—the one with the new tile business who had been expanding his locations and looking for a nationwide social media campaign to help him successfully roll out his new stores.

She had asked him about his client because she saw he was listed as Chuck's connection on LinkedIn. Chuck had chattered on and on about the great business he did with this client when she asked for an introduction, and he had said he would make an introduction, but that was three months ago. Each month she would ask, and each month he said he would "get around to it soon."

Meredith rooted around on her desk for the digital voice recorder, turned it on, pointed it at Chuck, and sat back at her desk. She watched him as he paced in front of the big-screen TV, complaining about the "new green and blue background" when, after all, he had requested it personally during his last round of changes.

Meredith had a habit of keeping a running tally of connections in her head. Her mental list had three columns: Clients, Prospects, and Referral Sources. Until she'd met Dan, she had everyone on her list as a potential referral source—people who would be open to making referrals to potential clients.

Chuck was quickly moving into the Client-only column. But that wasn't the only list she put Chuck on that day. After he finalized his changes and let her know his revised deadline, Meredith opened that week's assignment and put Chuck's name down at the top of the Taker column, especially after he ended the meeting asking if he could meet with her another day to "pick her brain" to explore, as he put it, "her gigantic network" with hopes she could introduce *him* to new business opportunities.

When she suggested that he could do the same for her, he weakly replied, "Well, I've tried, but I don't have a network like yours, so it's not really worthwhile." She was glad to put Chuck finally in the Taker category, which meant she would most likely not be meeting with him for an exchange of opportunities any time soon...if at all. She spent the rest of the day gaining a stronger and stronger awareness of the current makeup of her network, weeding out lots and lots of people.

Finally, Meredith was able to unwind with her last meeting of the day at Francisco's, a local bistro around the corner from her office. As Francisco himself poured her a home-brewed peach tea and buttered a hot, crisp Cuban roll, she sat admiring the wall art he had commissioned by a local painter with whom she had put him in touch.

"This place is really shaping up, Francisco," she said, savoring the flavor of the hot, buttered roll that melted in her mouth. "I can't believe you've only been open three months."

"All thanks to that YouTube channel you set up for us, Meredith." The old man smiled, sitting down next to her at the empty bar. "Last week I uploaded a video with one of our bartenders making a mojito from scratch, and oh my goodness, we had to order an extra shipment of rum for overnight delivery!"

Meredith smiled, catching herself blushing. "It doesn't hurt that the bartender in question looks just like a young Antonio Banderas!"

"You noticed, eh?" Francisco asked, as the two shared a laugh.

"So what was so urgent?" she asked playfully as he served her steaming sweet plantains and a small dish of cubed pork.

He winked and stood up from the bar. "Follow me and I'll show you."

She looked longingly at her dish but followed him nonetheless. The bistro was quiet this time of day, but she knew from experience that in only a few hours it would be bustling with live conga music and happy patrons milling about the bar and dining on the open-air patio out front.

"You remember I told you about the private dining room I was thinking about?" he asked, running a caramel finger through his bristly white hair.

"I better. We ran a contest on your Facebook page where fans could vote on their favorite layout."

"Very popular," he said. They came to a set of rough-hewn double doors and, with a devilish grin, Francisco opened it to reveal a cavernous space filled with warm terra cotta painted walls and a long, wooden table surrounded by at least a dozen chairs. "Only instead of a private dining room, I'm finding customers want to hold meetings here."

Meredith nodded silently as she admired the hammered-copper wall hangings and earthen water jugs on a weathered sideboard. "What a great place for a meeting!"

He turned and took her hands. "I'm glad you think so, Meredith. I wanted to make it available to you and other clients, free of charge, whenever you need it—as long as there are not paying customers wanting the space first! That would be your fault though, given your great marketing talent!" He winked at her and smiled.

Meredith's mind was already whirling. What a great opportunity to give clients or potential clients—a unique and new destination rather than just clustering around in her office or ordering coffee at the local café.

She immediately thought of Dan and the sweetheart deal he had with the local hotel, exchanging increased business and word-of-mouth advertising for a comfortable, convenient, and compatible offsite meeting room.

Immediately, Meredith put Francisco's name at the top of her *Exchanger* list.

· · · · · ·

Meredith felt at ease as she pulled her late-model Lexus into the hotel parking lot a few days later. Gone were her earlier hesitations, even doubts, about working with Dan.

Although she was still anxious to see where his "alternative networking theories"—or so she and Lance secretly called them—were leading, so far he had done something even more important—he had gotten her to change her perspective.

All week long, as she'd gone about tweeting and posting updates on her usual social media sites and returning phone calls and lunching with clients, she'd had a decidedly different attitude. She'd taken time to reflect before every meeting what she could learn about the person she was about to shake hands with, or speak with, or e-mail back and forth with.

During that week, she often found herself asking "big picture" questions, as Dan might call them:

- "Is this person aligned with my values? With my vision?"
- "Can we help each other? Or can they just help me?"
- "Are we a good fit?"
- "Will this connection matter, not just for me but for him/her?"
- "Will our connection and our knowledge, new and old, help
  others we know? In other words, could our respective or mutual success benefit others in their networks?"

Although it hadn't changed the number of appointments she made or went to, it had changed Meredith's outlook on the appointments she felt weren't up to snuff. Toward the end of the week, she found herself making fewer but better appointments.

She had also worked hard to whittle down her contact list, focusing on who was a Giver, a Taker, or an

Exchanger. The result was a revelation. She recalled three contacts in particular that had really surprised her.

Ariel was a Giver. She was forever bringing Meredith gift baskets or tokens of her affection in a very real, very personal way. But, Meredith noted, it was never in a really professional way. Ariel would throw out literally dozens of, as she put it, "possible" connections.

As a result, Meredith would find herself talking with literally dozens of people who had little or no possibility of using her services, nor did they know anyone else who might be interested in using them.

What's more, as giving as Ariel was, she was not a good receiver. Whenever Meredith tried to offer her something extra, such as an opportunity or movie tickets from another client, or even a meeting with another client, she quickly demurred. She preferred to see Meredith as a vendor, not a partner. For that reason, as generous as she was, she never quite made it to the Exchanger column.

Chuck, as she had assessed earlier, was a classic Taker. He talked a good game and was always up for jotting down one of the names she suggested as connections and having her introduce him to several people, but he never quite returned the favor. He was always going to message her with the e-mail address of that great gal who did his bookkeeping... but he failed to stay true to his word... The the name of that great and affordable caterer who specialized in breakfast meetings on the go was always on the tip of his tongue, but after working together for two years... it had never materialized.

Finally, she smiled as she realized that Francisco, her friend and ally all along, was an Exchanger. He was not only genuinely appreciative of what she'd done for him, but he was eager to exchange ideas, opinions, contacts, connections—and even a venue in which to incorporate them all!

But it wasn't just his generous offer that inspired her to call Francisco an Exchanger. It was his attitude. He was always open, enthusiastic about exchanging new ideas and information, just like she was. As Dan would no doubt put it, he was "a big picture person." Francisco and Meredith exchanged more than just opportunities—they shared the same vision and values.

Of all her most valued connections, Francisco had made it to the top of her list of five that Dan wanted her to identify for her "Primary Circle." As she parked, she looked down at her list and read the five names listed there silently to herself. A few were on the margins, but she was confident that all were good Exchangers according to Dan's definition.

· · · · · ·

Meredith heard polite chatter as she entered the same hotel conference room they'd used the previous week and smiled when she found Dan and Lance seated in the comfortable chairs. She poured herself coffee and joined them.

"So," Dan asked, "what did you guys think of this week's assignment?"

Lance cleared his throat and handed over a sticky note with only one name printed on it. "As you can see, I didn't do very well. My Primary Circle has only one name in it."

He shot Meredith an embarrassed grin and she nodded in support, giving him a *chin up* look.

"What did you find so hard about it, Lance?" Dan asked.

"Well, I knew it wouldn't be easy, but I have to admit it would have been a lot easier if I hadn't met you!"

They all chuckled as Lance explained, "I mean, if someone had just asked me to list five Exchangers, I would have done so easily. That is, until you gave me a better definition of what a true Exchanger does; that made it harder. It appears that most of my contacts are, frankly, Takers."

"Mine too," Meredith interjected, handing her list over to Dan when Lance had run out of steam. "I had trouble whittling it down at first, but I realized that not many of my contacts are actually 'connections that matter,' given your definition last week."

Dan took the assignments and nodded, barely glancing at the names before he slid them onto the low-slung coffee table beside him. Meredith and Lance shared a look and, Dan being Dan, he smiled, catching them.

"The names aren't really important to me," he said, leaning forward in his seat. "What's important was the exercise of seeing the people you know through a fresh lens—an objective, fresh pair of eyes.

"Most people," he went on, "get hung up with the external trappings of the people they already know, making huge assumptions and sweeping conclusions about people in their lives. Everyone has an *authentic* story that lives below the surface of their job, their hairstyle, and the clothes they wear. It's your unique story that evolves from your *why* we talked about earlier. Have people in your Primary Circle who are Exchangers or have the potential of becoming Exchangers and you can generate new conversations and find people you already know who have similar values and purpose around what they are trying to create in their companies, local communities, or even the world."

Meredith thought of this as Dan paused to let his latest "lesson" sink in. As much as Ariel was a Giver and Chuck a Taker, she would still hate to stop working with them, connecting with them. Would that make her a Taker if she cut them off simply because they hadn't made it into her Primary Circle?

Dan added, as if he read her mind, "Just because you put someone into a category that is not that of an Exchanger, they don't have to be removed from your network altogether. You can move them to your Secondary Circle where you connect less frequently or even your Tertiary Circle where you check in maybe once a year. The important thing is that you have your Primary Circle in place so that you can leverage those *exchanging* relationships into great and ongoing opportunities."

"So how do we get to know their stories better?" she asked Dan. "I mean, I'm thinking in particular of a few people who I thought were great contacts but aren't, but could be... how do I find out for sure?"

Dan beamed. "I'm really glad you asked that, Meredith, because that leads me right into next week's assignment. Before you reach out to any contacts this week, before you pick up the phone to call them or click your mouse to e-mail them or tweet at them or race downstairs to meet them, I want you to spend a couple of minutes 'researching' them."

"How do we do that, Dan?" Lance asked.

Dan shrugged and Meredith could tell that he figured a part of the lesson was for them to find out for themselves. "How do you do anything, Lance?" Dan said instead. "Google them. Look at their profile on LinkedIn. Look at their connections, their Web site, their blog, their Twitter, Google+, or Facebook page—the races they ran in or the charity events they attended or... the wedding photos they have on their Tumblr site.

"We think we know the people we work with, but we don't. We could know more. It's all out there, and the more you know about the social side of someone, the better you can connect to that part of them—the part that is human and wants to connect back at a deeper, more sustainable level. That's what building social capital is all about—not just for you—but for the people with whom you partner as well.

"For instance, Meredith, chances are you could look closer at each of the five names you currently have on your list and discover that some of these folks don't really share your vision or your values. They only seem like good Exchangers. By the same token, you could probably find folks just outside of your Primary Circle—maybe somebody in your Secondary Circle—who does in fact align more closely with the way you do business. But you have to know their stories first. Dig below the surface of what you think you know."

Meredith liked that—digging below the surface. As much time as she spent with her clients, contacts, and connections, what did she really know about them?

Dan went on, "The more you get to know your contacts, I want you to start having conversations with your potential partners to explore new possibilities and see if you can have conversations with more substance. Skip the small talk and dig a little deeper to sincerity.

"Given that making connections that matter is about finding people with shared values, interactions must be substantive and values-connecting, not superficial. Part of this means being a bit more open and authentic than you may be used to being. Part of this is asking great questions that take your conversations to a deeper level. It's also about having more conscious conversations."

Meredith nodded, watching Lance do the same. "That could take some getting used to," she admitted. "I tend to keep people at arm's length, if only out of respect for them."

"Absolutely," Dan agreed. "We all do, but this is about making deeper, not more, connections. Let your instincts guide you. If you think a connection is strong enough, the right questions can only strengthen it. You'll see. It's like a wall comes down and opens you both up to a new relationship. That's all we're looking for here—newer, deeper relationships."

Meredith was thinking of Francisco, and how much deeper their connection could be if she could just get him to talk about himself a little more: his background, his family, his energy, and why community is so important to him.

She made a mental note to do so, but Lance was already thinking ahead.

"So," he asked, avoiding Meredith's eyes, "are we ready to be introduced to some of your contacts, Dan?"

Meredith smiled slyly. She knew what Lance was getting at. His circle was empty; no doubt he wanted to fill it with some "proven" connections from Dan!

For his part, Dan smiled humbly but shook his head firmly. "Not yet," he said, standing to signal the meeting was over. "Keep digging deeper with your current list first."

Dan started to gather up his things but then stopped suddenly. "Oh, I almost forgot something. Your network is dynamic. What I mean by that is your circles will expand and contract. It's all about being ready, willing, and able to exchange. You see, some people will be too busy transitioning in a job or moving, to name a few examples. Perhaps they are not *able* currently to be part of your Primary or Secondary Circles. Just remain flexible."

With that final instruction, Dan pulled out the familiar two white sheets of paper with the tips for this session and finished packing up his computer, notepad, and pen. He hugged both Meredith and Lance before he left them sitting, silently staring at their respective guides.

....

DAN'S THIRD-LESSON TIPS

✓ Digging below the surface is all about having conscious conversations with your potential Primary or Secondary Circle partners to determine where they best fit in your network.

✓ Listen with your eyes. Determine who should be in your network by what people do rather than what they say they will do.

✓ Be curious and do your research. Before you jump in headfirst in making your connections, find out more about them—especially through their social media channels.

✓ Your circles are dynamic. You will find that people will come and go in your circles. Remain flexible.

✓ Be prepared by constantly keeping an open eye for new circle partners. Keep a mental list and written list of Givers, Takers, and Exchangers.

HAVE YOUR AUTHENTIC STORY READY TO GO

L ANCE COULD BARELY believe his ears. This was it! Dan was finally ready to make the introductions that he and Meredith had both been waiting for. Clearly, as they sat in the cozy hotel conference room exactly one week later, Meredith was disbelieving as well.

"Are you sure this isn't a trick?" she asked as Lance nodded furiously.

Dan chuckled, sitting back in his chair. "Now, why would I trick you two?"

Meredith shot Lance a *what now*? look. Lance grinned. "Well, Dan, it's just that you made it sound like we'd need to find the holy grail before we could get a connection out of you, and it's only been a couple of weeks."

Dan smiled back, but his tone was serious as he replied, "I said I'd make an introduction, Lance. What you do with it is up to you."

Lance wasn't sure he liked Dan's tone. So far, every week there had been a lesson. Was the connection this week's lesson? He listened as Dan said, "Okay, Meredith, for you I've got a great contact. Her name is Carol Livingston and she's VP of social media marketing for Running Start."

"The sneaker company?" Meredith asked, sitting up in her seat a little taller.

Dan nodded and handed Meredith a business card before turning his attention to Lance. "And Lance, you're in for a big treat. It just so happens that Peter James, one of my clients, works for the Principle Group's restaurant division."

Lance's eyes grew wide. When Meredith shot him a questioning glance, he quickly explained, "Principle Group runs the Papa's Pasta Parlor chain. Wow, Dan, this could be *huge* for me."

Dan smiled humbly and stood. "Both Carol and Peter are expecting you, and I've done my best to make the proper introductions. From here on in, it's up to you two. I wish you the best and look forward to hearing how it goes next week."

Dan left the room and Lance sat stunned, staring at the business card Dan had handed him before leaving.

"Papa's Pasta Parlor, huh?" Meredith said, admiring the familiar green and red logo in the corner of the card. "Lance, just think what could happen if your firm landed that account."

"I can't," Lance confessed.

Meredith snorted playfully as she pulled her iPhone out of her stuffed purse. "Why not?" she asked.

"It's too intimidating!"

She shook her head and smiled as she began dialing numbers. "Who are you calling?" he asked.

"Dan's connection, of course," she whispered, holding up a manicured finger as someone answered on the other line. "Yes, hello, Meredith Mathers for Carol Livingston, please."

There was a pause before Meredith replied, "Yes, I was referred by Dan Paterno, of—oh, you do? Great! Okay, well certainly; tomorrow at 4:00 P.M. sounds perfect. Yes, I have the address right here. Thanks so much and I'm really looking forward to it."

"That was easy," Lance exclaimed as Meredith made a quick notation in her phone's calendar feature before sliding it back in her purse.

"Dan's name really opened that door, I'll tell you. I was this close to getting shut down before I mentioned him, then it was as if the floodgates of happiness opened."

Lance nodded, turning the Papa's Pasta Parlor business card over and over in his fingers. "Your turn," Meredith nudged gently.

He grinned but with a sour feeling in his stomach. This was why he'd agreed to meet with Dan in the first place—not so much for his connections but for the confidence to capitalize on those connections.

At the moment, he was feeling supremely unconfident.

Still, there was no time like the present, and he knew Meredith was eager to leave and start preparing for her meeting. If she left him to his own devices, Lance knew—and he supposed Meredith did as well—he might never follow through.

Before he could lose his nerve, Lance slid out his phone and dialed the number on the card. It was a direct line to Peter James's office, and the receptionist answered with a clipped, "Hello and welcome to Papa's Pasta Parlor marketing division, how can I direct your call?"

"Peter James, please," said Lance.

"I'll direct your call," said the woman, causing Lance to panic. He'd assumed that, like Meredith, he'd make an appointment with Peter's secretary.

"Peter James speaking," said a gruff voice.

Lance stammered, "Mr. James, yes, this is Lance Hardy, I'm a friend of Dan Paterno's?"

"Yes?" said Peter James briskly, the name clearly not opening the kinds of doors Meredith had led him to believe—at least, not yet.

Lance shot Meredith a *what now?* glance and said, "Yes, well, Dan thought that maybe you and I should get together and talk over some possibilities . . ."

Meredith gave him a thumbs-up sign, but Lance wasn't so sure. Peter said, "Sounds good to me, Lance. How about this afternoon? I usually break for lunch about 2:00 P.M. I could meet you in the corporate cafeteria downstairs. I'll be the only one wearing a tie!"

"That'd be fine, sir, yes," Lance said to a dial tone.

"Yikes," he groaned to Meredith as they stood to leave the room. "I was hoping for a little more time to prepare."

Meredith gave him a conspiratorial pat on the shoulder. "Sometimes, Lance, more time just means more time to worry."

. . . . . .

Peter James wasn't kidding. Not only was he the only employee in the Principle Group cafeteria wearing a tie, but he was older than the other employees gathered there by a good twenty years.

"Welcome to the Kiddy Zone," said Peter gruffly as the two shook hands after Lance made his way over to Peter's table in the corner.

With a napkin still in his hand and food still in his mouth, Peter offered Lance a seat. Lance's stomach rumbled; he had assumed they'd have lunch and he hadn't had anything to eat before their early afternoon meeting.

"Is everyone here so young?" Lance asked, taking a seat and eyeing the garlic bread on Peter's plate.

"Most are younger," Peter complained, pushing his plate away. It was clear he'd already eaten and was eager to get the meeting started. "So, Lance, how can I help you today?"

Lance was nearly thrown by the question. He had assumed Dan's name would immediately clue Peter in to what he was there for, and why. "W-w-well, Mr. James," Lance stammered, "I work for Hospitality, Inc. As you may know, we specialize in doing accounting for chains like Papa's Pasta Parlor and—"

"I don't," Peter said, staring back at Lance.

"I'm sorry?"

"I don't know that you specialize in doing accounting for fast-food chains."

His tone was pleasant, his jaw firm, his eyes clear and bracing. And yet, there was something...confrontational...about Peter's statement. Lance thought for a moment and said, "Well, now you do!"

He was hoping for a little cocky humor, but the joke fell flat. He and Peter simply weren't connecting. The vibe was awkward and growing more so by the minute.

"I suppose I should start over," Lance hemmed.

Peter shook his head and said brusquely, "How about I try? What brings you here today, Lance, really?"

Despite Peter's abrupt tone, the question was a good one, and sincere. Lance risked an equally sincere answer: "To be honest, I've never eaten in the Papa's Pasta Parlor cafeteria before!"

He'd meant it as a joke, a way to diffuse the obvious tension this abrupt and unfortunate meeting had created, but either Peter James wasn't a joking man or Lance just didn't tell jokes very well.

Peter nodded and gathered his things. "I appreciate you coming to see me today, Lance. I hope that next time we meet, we can both be better prepared."

. . . . . .

Dan chuckled when, the following week, Lance related the story in an admittedly pitiful tone. Quickly apologizing, Dan said, "Lance, trust me, I'm not laughing at you, just with you. We've all been there, right, Meredith?"

"Yeah, like last week," Meredith said despondently.

Dan arched one eyebrow and, as he turned to look at her, so did Lance. "But I thought your meeting got off to such a great start," he said to her.

Meredith merely groaned. "Yes, the meeting got off to a great start, but eventually I discovered I just didn't have anything in common with the woman. Of course, it's not her fault."

Lance chuckled. "Maybe you should have met with her secretary instead."

Meredith nodded. Dan interjected, "Actually, Lance, you make a good point. Sometimes it's better to have a meeting with someone you click with, even if you don't necessarily have something to offer each other—other than good conversation, that is."

Lance chuckled. "Actually, Dan, after Peter James left, I *did* have a good conversation with Jack, the guy who ran the salad bar."

"Salad bar?" asked Meredith.

"Hey, I said I'd never eaten at the Papa's Pasta Parlor cafeteria before. I wasn't going home without crossing that item off my bucket list!"

This time, Dan seemed to be laughing. "What did you two talk about?" he asked.

"Who, me and Jack, the salad bar guy?" Lance asked. When Dan nodded, Lance admitted, "I asked him why everybody who worked at the Pasta Parlor seemed so young. Jack said that their recruiting staff was twice the size of any other department, and that everyone who worked there was pretty much fresh out of college, but that turnover was extremely high. I asked him why he worked there, and he said he was working his way through school, majoring in, guess what?...economics. I handed him my card and told him to call me when he graduates next semester! I want to see if I can help him get an interview with my company."

Meredith clapped her hands appreciatively as Dan nodded. "See there, Lance, you made a connection after all."

As he finished his story, Lance realized that he'd learned much more from Jack than he had by meeting with Peter. Dan seemed to be in agreement.

"Now, let's think about that for a minute, Lance," said Dan. "Why do you think you got along so well with that cafeteria worker, Jack, and not so well with the executive I set you up with?"

Lance replied, "I can't really tell you. Maybe I didn't feel so pressured once Peter left the cafeteria or I didn't expect anything from Jack. And, really, he didn't know me from Adam or that I ran a company that might one day hire him. We weren't there trying to get anything from one another, we were just there to…make a connection."

Dan nodded knowingly. "Going into a first meeting without someone with any expectations is tough to do but much more beneficial. More specifically, having the belief that *anything is possible* is the best way to approach a meeting. This belief will drive a better attitude and set of behaviors. I have seen, for example, where an encounter with no expectations has lead to one of the biggest deals of someone's career. Both of you, I'm sorry that these connections were a little out of your comfort zone. Peter and Carol are both great connections, and I sincerely want you to follow them up with a second meeting…just not yet."

Meredith and Lance looked at each other, confused. "So, wait," Meredith asked. "That first meeting was…a setup?"

Dan shook his head fiercely and waved his hands in surrender. "Hardly, gang; none of us have time for setups. However, I wanted you to meet with two connections who were outside of your comfort zones so you would realize how important it is to be prepared under any conditions. Connections can be made anywhere, anytime. And although we've been working hard at exploring your current connections to dig deeper, today I'd like to talk about the importance of having your authentic story ready to go, especially for situations where you are less comfortable, like what happened this week. One way to form powerful human connections is through stories. Powerful, strong, human, personal stories."

"Like what?" joked Meredith. "Nursery rhymes?"

Dan wagged his finger playfully. "You know better, Meredith. These are *your* stories, why you do what you do, what you can do for others, and what makes you tick. Lance, you said you got stumped when Peter asked why you were there that day. If you'd had your authentic story ready, I guarantee you could have told it simply, easily, sincerely, and the meeting would have had a drastically different outcome. Do you believe me?"

Lance nodded. "I believe that if I'd been as comfortable around Peter as I was with Jack, then yes, I would have made a more powerful connection."

Meredith nodded. "I agree. But we can't just wait for the other person to make us feel comfortable. We have to create a comfortable atmosphere. I think telling stories that create connections can help us do that."

Dan nodded eagerly now. "Sometimes you have to prime the pump a little, Meredith. The more confident and comfortable you are at making connections and sharing engaging stories that resonate with those you meet, the more powerful those connections become. I recommend you have your stories thought out and ready to go when you meet new people so the connections you make are thoughtful and focused on your mutual stories. Valuable connections are all around you and many times the difference between making or missing a mutually valuable connection is your ability simply to articulate who you are, what journey you are on, why you are on it, and what you need to take another step forward. When you have your story ready, you are also more prepared to draw out the stories of others because you know what to ask."

"So how can we do that, Dan?" Lance asked.

"Well, first of all, you need to prepare your stories. They start with your vision and passion. We talked about your individual visions and passions earlier. Then you tie these into a specific experience you have had that illustrates more *who* you are over *what* you do for a living. Lance, you already said you connected so well with Jack, the cafeteria worker, because you had no expectations of each other, no pressure. But weren't you happy when you heard that he was studying economics?"

"Absolutely," Lance replied.

"Why?" Dan probed.

"Because suddenly we had something in common and I could help him."

"Exactly!" Dan and Meredith shouted at the same time.

"Is this a good example of a story?" Lance asked hopefully.

"Yes," Dan added. "You shared *how* you helped a soon-to-be college graduate effectively and in doing that, you showed more about *who* you are—someone who cares about others and takes the time to go out of your way to help. Your story shows others that you are someone who would make a good circle partner."

Dan paused a moment before turning to Meredith and asking, "So, Meredith, how do you think your story might sound? Don't recite it for me yet. You'll have all week to work on these so no pressure, but…what would you want to tell me if we'd never met?"

Meredith shot a glance toward Lance before turning back to Dan and extending a hand. "I'm Meredith," she announced confidently. "And I love to help young people get better starts in their careers. This began after I helped my brother, who was having tremendous difficulty getting into law school, study for the LSAT—Law School Admission Test—and because of my help, he ended up not only getting a great score, but he got into his dream school. Since then I have developed a passion for helping any young person when I can. With that passion, my vision is to create a wonderful team of young, up-and-coming social media sensations who work with me to help companies jump successfully into this new world of social media. With this stellar team of seasoned veterans with top strategy skills that I have developed combined with the bold energy of a team of talented and collaborative young social media professionals, my firm has the differentiator that creates a competitive edge and, as a result, attracts the most amazing client list possible."

Dan leaned forward and high-fived Meredith. "Good job!" He smiled and turned to Lance. "Your turn, pal."

He watched Lance squirm in his chair but then sit forward, clear his throat, and begin. "I love to help family-owned restaurateurs blend their love of family and good food with great, state-of-the-art restaurant designs so they can compete in one of the most competitive marketplaces out there. My vision is to expand my practice into other locations around the country so that hundreds of similar families will be able to grow their restaurants generation after generation. In turn, people who are served by those families will experience amazing cuisines as well as world-class service and, most of all, a loving family environment."

Lance stopped. He waited for Dan to speak. Dan's head was down, cupped in his hands, making both Lance and Meredith grow anxious with doubt. Then, suddenly, Dan lifted his head. He smiled, flooding Lance's heart with pure relief. "Good," he finally exhaled. "You should both now be much more prepared for unexpected connection opportunities in the future."

The three of them ended their meeting with Dan's usual dissemination of tip sheets. Lance and Meredith were particularly excited to move forward by first making sure they absorbed what they learned from their current session.

DAN'S FOURTH-LESSON TIPS

✓ Great stories build connections as people identify with your experiences on a personal level.

✓ Be bold and confident. Share your story and then ask your connections
to share theirs. Sharing your stories also builds rapport and trust.

✓ Acknowledge and share your appreciation for one another to create
further connection.

✓ Allow yourself to help others. Don't feel as if you're being too generous or giving away too much with nothing in exchange. Keeping score won't do you good.

✓ Creating your authentic story is about combining your passion with your vision and connecting these to a story that shares powerfully who you are rather than what you do or have done. Work at it until you have your authentic story ready to share.

GIVE FIRST

MEREDITH WAS READYING HERSELF for that week's meeting with Dan when her cell phone trilled an alert for an incoming text message. "Sorry, folks," Dan had written only a few moments earlier. "A family emergency is forcing me to postpone this week's meeting but not this week's lesson: Give First."

Meredith looked at the phone, half-relieved she wouldn't have to trek halfway across town but more than a little disappointed that she wouldn't be able to get more introductions. In fact, she and Lance had made a pact that this was the week they would pin Dan down on giving them more introductions to people in his network.

A follow-up e-mail explained: "This week, you should first go back and connect with one of your Primary Circle partners and give first by asking what is one thing that partner would like your help with. By giving first to those key people in your network, you set up a powerful environment for a reciprocal relationship, rather than one that is one-sided. If you have chosen the right Primary Circle partners, you will then find that your efforts have fallen on fertile soil for continuous networking, meaningful connection, and creating an exchanging relationship. Also, download this week's guide."

Meredith responded with best wishes for a quick resolution to Dan's family emergency, then sat back at her desk. Her office was pleasant with bamboo wallpaper and a light green and brown palette of colors and accessories. A large picture window faced the industrial park below, where a small but beautiful open space with benches and bronze sculptures by a local artist was bordered by a row of majestic oak trees.

Finding herself with a free hour—make that nearly two hours, given the commute to Dan's favorite hotel—wasn't something Meredith experienced often. Instinctively, she thought of the dozen and one things she could, possibly *should*, be doing. But she'd devoted herself to Dan's program for the last month, and she wanted to make sure it took by following all of his lessons.

Dan had given her and Lance no reason to doubt him so far, and she didn't want to lose a week's worth of solid work simply because nobody was looking. She had ignored a flood of that morning's e-mails and her workaholic tendencies and instead focused on what

Dan had sent her: "By giving first to those key people in your network, you set up a powerful environment for a reciprocal relationship, rather than one that is one-sided. Also, download this week's guide."

First and foremost, Meredith considered herself a giving person. That's why she'd gotten into social media in the first place. It was the first time in the history of marketing and promotion where giving was in the actual job description! That is, if you did it right.

She wondered, though, in her eagerness to make strong connections if she always thought of the other person. If she had to put herself in a category, would she assess herself as a Giver, a Taker, or an Exchanger? Although she would have loved to consider herself an Exchanger, and in most cases she was, like many small-business owners she was sometimes forced to be a Taker. It didn't happen often but often enough to give her pause with Dan's new assignment.

Feeling slightly sheepish, Meredith turned back to her e-mail from that morning. Dan wanted her to give to an existing contact, not someone new, and the fastest, simplest, most random way to do that was to see who'd written her that day.

Seventy-four e-mails. That's how many she'd received since logging off of her computer the night before. Seventy-four names to help, to give to, but the minute she saw an e-mail from her colleague Anne asking for a little hiring advice, she made her choice.

She e-mailed Anne back and set up a quick lunch date. Before they met, however, Meredith stood up from her desk and headed out the door. She had some work to do in her HR Department before her meeting.

· · · · · ·

"So, how's the entrepreneurial life treating you, Anne?" Meredith asked as she sat down on a bench in the small park between their two offices. Anne was a former employee who, several months earlier, had made the leap to form her own boutique advertising agency.

"I wish I could say I was hiring for growth," said Anne, a petite blonde in white slacks and a navy blazer. "It's just hard to find good team members who you know are team players."

Meredith nodded and joined Anne in line at Doug's Dogs and Donuts, a popular lunch cart that parked in the park each morning and left each afternoon. They'd had many lunches there when Anne still worked for Meredith.

"So, tell me a little about what you're looking for," Meredith said as they sat back down with the daily lunch special: a hot dog, soda, and a cake donut for $2.99. Meredith bought, taking Dan's lesson to *give first* literally.

"I need two people, actually," Anne confessed, wiping a smidge of ketchup off her lower lip before setting the second half of her hot dog back in its shiny foil tray. "One is for an administrative position, and the other is creative."

Meredith nodded. "In my experience," she said gently, "creative support can be as valuable as creative-creative."

Anne blushed. "No, you're right, Meredith. I'm just trying to prioritize what's going to help me with my current client load and keep the folks I do have happy while filling the pipeline for the next few months."

Meredith nodded. How many times had she been in Anne's shoes? Stuck between a rock and a hard place and an unpaid invoice or two away from closing her doors—and her very dream—forever?

Meredith opened her valise and pulled out a thin stack of resumes. She'd highlighted the contact information on each of the six she'd brought along, and pointed this out as she handed them to Anne.

"What are these?" the young entrepreneur asked earnestly.

"Last month I hired a new assistant. She's wonderful, but...so were these six people. The decision was a hard one, and I'd be proud to recommend any one of these people."

Anne looked up from the slim pile and asked, "Don't you want to hold onto these?"

Meredith nodded, then grinned. "Sure I do." Company policy was to hold onto resumes for at least six months and to hire, if possible, based on a previous talent search rather than starting from scratch. As a former employee, Anne knew this all too well.

Anne frowned, looking down at the resumes. "Er... I don't know how to say this, Meredith, but will these folks even respond if I mention that my starting salary is at least five grand lower than yours?"

Meredith smiled. "Not all, Anne, but it's worth a shot. Like I said, we began the initial candidate search a few months back, so if any of these folks are still available, my bet is they'll be willing to negotiate. But more important, the reason they're in this pile in the first place is because they impressed me as team players, folks who—like you, like me—come to work for more than a paycheck. So I think you'll find a gem in this pile, trust me."

Anne smiled, looking reassured. Meredith felt good. She'd been sincerely disappointed she hadn't been able to hire all the candidates who'd made it to the final round before choosing her last assistant. She was glad that, at the very least, one of them might now find a job with someone like Anne, who would not only appreciate but reward a solid team player.

Anne filed the resumes away in her own distressed leather messenger bag before looking up sheepishly. She swept a blond lock behind her ear and said, "Well, that takes care of the support person, hopefully, but about the creative…"

Anne let her voice drift off and Meredith rested a hand reassuringly on her shoulder. "I don't have any resumes for that, unfortunately, but what I can do is what I do best: tap into my contacts. Before this meeting I put a call out on Twitter, LinkedIn, Facebook, and through Google+, and when I get back to the office I'll get on the phones and start working my personal connections, business owners or recruiters or other creatives who may be between jobs. Don't worry, Anne. We'll find you somebody."

Anne looked grateful but still tense. "I know talk is cheap," Meredith added as they both stood and tossed their foil wrappers in the nearest trashcan, "but I care about you and your success, Anne. I've been where you are, and although it's not always pleasant, it's a learning experience."

"But why are you doing all this for a competitor, Meredith?"

Meredith shrugged. "I'd like to think we're friends first, Anne, competitors second." Anne smiled and nodded in agreement.

In the car on the quick drive to Lance's office, where she had an afternoon appointment, she spoke to friends and colleagues via the Bluetooth built into her steering wheel. In addition to the resumes she had handed Anne, she was fairly certain she had a few leads in the creative department as well.

"Hey, do you mind if we walk a little?" Lance asked, meeting her at her car as she pulled into the employee parking lot of Hospitality, Inc.

Meredith, who had come fresh from her lunch date with Anne and still had her walking shoes on, smiled and said, "Great idea!"

"I've just been sitting all day," Lance explained as they started onto the paved track that surrounded the commercial park where Lance's building was located.

"So, what did you think of Dan's assignment?" Meredith asked as they settled into a brisk, if comfortable, pace.

"I was a little offended at first," he answered, mirroring Meredith's own initial *how dare he suggest I'm not a giver* reaction, "but then I realized he was right. We could all stand to give first and receive second, you know? And since I don't have a huge list of contacts like you, the only folks I could give to were on my inner circle."

He gave her a playful nudge as he continued, "Then I got to thinking about last week's meeting with Dan's contact, the grump at Papa's Pasta Parlor? And how I'd written it off, but then I remembered Jack, the kid in the cafeteria. He'd given me his cell phone number, which I figured I'd never use, but I called him and he answered right away. I asked him if he was doing any interning, and he said he'd considered it but with class and work, he wasn't sure he'd have the time. I asked him if it'd be okay to call around on his behalf, maybe find him an opportunity where he could get credit for his next semester. He seemed pretty jazzed, so I've been working on that all day."

Meredith was impressed. Not only had Lance shown some major initiative calling this kid up out of the blue like that, but he seemed genuinely excited about it.

"Any luck?" she asked.

He shrugged. "I think I got him a slot doing night auditing for Barry's Bistro downtown."

"Yeah?"

"They're a client and I know they're really active with the university Jack is going to, so...they seemed excited about the prospect. I think Jack did, too, when I told him. They should meet next week to iron out all the formalities."

"Another Italian place, huh?" Meredith joked. "Poor kid's gonna get typecast."

"Well, at least this one's moving him out of the cafeteria. My client tells me most interns get hired on before they graduate, so...here's hoping."

They walked for a little while until Meredith asked, "So, I have to ask, just between you and me, what do you think you'll get out of this partnership with Jack?"

Lance smirked. "You first, Meredith. How will moving heaven and earth to find two employees for your competitor help you?"

Meredith thought for a few steps before responding. "I like Anne and I've been where she is. We worked well together and I think once she's up and running and clear of her first few years of business, we'll be able to partner on something. What's more, she seemed immensely grateful for what I'd done and I don't think you can go wrong with generating that kind of goodwill."

"Same with me," he confessed. "I just liked Jack and I felt for him. He seemed so smart and quick and motivated, and there he was stuck in the cafeteria, you know? I know we've all been there, we've all paid our dues, but so many people have helped me along the way to where I am now so I thought I'd try to be one of those people to him."

Meredith nodded; his answer was so sincere, how could it be wrong?

"I wonder, though," she offered, "what Dan will think of it."

Lance smirked. "I guess we'll have to wait until next week to find out!"

The two spent the rest of the hour going through Dan's guide, which Meredith had printed out for both herself and Lance. They were very happy to see they had done well with the task of giving first, even though Dan had not been with them to set the foundation for their efforts. They agreed this task was easier than they thought and that giving had lots of intrinsic rewards they had not expected.

DAN'S FIFTH-LESSON TIPS

✓ You must first connect by showing you are a Giver versus a Taker.

✓ Once you give first, you set into action a potential for exchange and build your skills as an Exchanger.

✓ Choose at least one person a month to give something to—time, treasures, talents, or thoughts are all options. It could be volunteering your time, mentoring someone, or sending someone information you believe they would benefit from knowing. It could also look like sponsoring something by offering financial support. Be creative with your giving.

✓ Give wisely. Give not to receive but to offer value. Giving wisely is about giving to someone you strongly believe would benefit from your gift, someone who will appreciate your gift and be likely to either reciprocate now or in the future to you or someone else.

✓ To get started, all you have to do is ask one of your partners what one thing they would like your help with. A very simple move on your part will set a foundation for a powerful environment.

UPGRADE YOUR NETWORK— FIVE LEVELS OF EXCHANGE

"WOW," Dan exclaimed the following week after Lance and Meredith had summarized their "Give First" lesson. "I was worried that I was letting you down by canceling last minute like that, but...it seems you went above and beyond the call of duty on this one."

Lance smiled, basking for a moment in Dan's enthusiasm. "So," Dan added, "any updates for me?"

"I'm glad to announce that Anne hired one of the support staff she needed from the stack of resumes I handed her," Meredith said. "And she's got interviews next week with two creative staffers from the connections I wrote to on Twitter and Facebook."

Lance was suitably impressed with Meredith's experiment in giving, as was Dan. When it was his turn, Lance explained, "Jack was approved for the internship at Barry's Bistro. He'll be doing their books at night and getting college credit toward his MBA, so it won't affect his job with the Pasta Parlor chain or his GPA. He's pretty stoked about it. Truth be told, so am I. I'm hoping that, one day, he'll come work for Hospitality, Inc."

"Now you're talking, Lance," Dan exclaimed, standing from his seat with an approving nod. "I'm glad to see you both not only got into the spirit of giving but were so happy and enthusiastic about it. Truly, the sign of a real Exchanger is one who is sincere and generous with his or her connections. You really can't fake the goodwill that fuels a solid, ongoing exchange between two great connections."

Dan was pacing in front of a tall stand set up next to the dry erase board at the back of the room. To follow his movements, Lance had to shift slightly in his chair. The stand held a giant sketch pad. On the first page, written in black marker, were the words *The Five Levels of Exchange.*

As Dan paused in front of the pad, Meredith cleared her throat and asked, "So, Dan, we're on Week Six of your little program now. Do you think we're finally ready to meet some more of your connections?"

Dan smiled. "I know you think you're ready, Meredith, and certainly you and Lance are poised to make powerful connections in the near future. Look how well you both did with the giving experiment, and how much it meant to you both. But now I propose something even more specific, something more hands-on that you can use to make meaningful connections that matter."

He paused, looking from the title on the sketch pad first to where Lance, then Meredith sat. "Just imagine what kinds of meetings you could have if you were an expert at taking any good potential Primary Circle partner through what I call the Five Levels of Exchange."

Meredith gave Lance a look. He asked, "Is that like Six Sigma?"

"Actually, Lance, it's a model I created that identifies the evolution of the most effective exchanges successful circle partners could offer one another. Going through this process moves building your network from a haphazard and often unconscious activity into a much more conscious and proactive process.

"So in today's lesson, I'm going to teach you the Five Levels of the Exchange."

Meredith and Lance exchanged looks before quickly pulling out their messenger bags for a way to take notes. Meredith was quick to retrieve her iPad, but Lance took a little longer to get his laptop up and running, a blank Word document finally filling the screen.

When they were both ready, Dan turned to the next page in the giant sketch pad. The words *Level 1: Social Exchange* were written on the page.

Dan pointed to them and said, "So, let's start with Level 1, or what I call 'Social Exchange.' This step is the foundation of building a strong relationship. You may also think of it as emotional intelligence, which is the ability to understand emotions and use them to promote emotional and intellectual growth in yourself and others.

"People are increasingly receptive to emotional honesty, and they're looking for someone who not only says what he or she really feels but is also an empathic listener. Emotional support builds trust and naturally allows the relationship to progress along the Exchange Model."

After a slight pause, Dan flipped to the next page. It read *Level 2: Information Exchange.* He began: "Once at least some kind of emotional exchange has been established, people are more willing to volunteer information. But let's face it, people are overwhelmed with data and information. Think of all the sources you yourself have from which to gather information. The key here is useful but easy-to-obtain information versus valuable, not-as-well-known facts and statistics."

Lance looked to Meredith, who was busy typing. Before Dan could continue, he cleared his throat and asked, "Well, what type of information, Dan? Can you give us a for instance?"

"Sure," Dan said, turning to them both. "You both just engaged in an extreme case of information exchange in the Give First exercise. Meredith gave those resumes, based on her Level 1 Social Exchange with Anne. And you, Lance, gave information and contact numbers for a valuable internship to Jack based on your earlier Social Exchange in the cafeteria at Papa's

Pasta Parlor. But information can be anything: a tip, a review, a business card, a Web link. That's the type of information we're talking about here."

On the following page were printed the words *Level 3: Knowledge-Wisdom Exchange*. Dan said, "Now, the next natural progression in relationship-building is knowledge. So I called Level 3 *Knowledge-Wisdom Exchange*."

"But, didn't we just cover that with *Information Exchange*, Dan?" Meredith asked before Lance could form the words.

Dan replied patiently. "There's actually a pretty big difference between knowledge and information. Information is typically pure data and facts; knowledge involves a personal experience, lessons learned, experiences, insights, and ideas.

"So, for example, if you give someone a tip, the name of an event you heard of but have not attended, or articles you have heard about but have not read, you are sharing information. Knowledge support, on the other hand, signifies a growing level of trust. Examples of knowledge-sharing could be experiences shared in mastermind groups or mentoring relationships. So, for instance, Lance, all you gave Jack so far is information: a contact at the college, a chance at an internship, the connection to make it happen. But let's say you really find yourself clicking with this kid and he pursues a relationship and begins exchanging experiences he has had and you share your insights and experiences that complement his. Well, your conversation could evolve into a knowledge exchange where you mentor him and take him under your wing."

Lance nodded toward Dan and chuckled, "Hmm, why does that sound familiar?"

They all laughed. "Exactly, we're having a knowledge exchange right now. But you can see how if you didn't trust me or I didn't trust you, we all might be a little less forthcoming with the type or amount of knowledge we convey. If you are doing this correctly, it adds an element of wisdom. Here, you are sharing that 20 percent that can yield an 80 percent return. Best-practice-sharing is an example of wisdom support."

Lance raced to type in Dan's words as Meredith did the same. The rustling of paper against paper caught his attention, and Lance risked a rare glance up from his laptop. Dan had flipped the last sheet of paper over to a new one.

Level 4: Connection Exchange was written on the next page. Dan pointed to it and said, "Connecting two people you know who do not know one another is leveraging your network, creating a ripple effect for those you connect as well as yourself. If you have made a strong connection through a great introduction, the people you connect will remember you for this and you will grow your social capital."

The final page said *Level 5: Opportunity Exchange*. Dan pointed to this page with particular pride. "Finally, gang, we get to Level 5 or what I call the 'Opportunity Exchange.' Here is your chance to be recommended or introduced to a wonderful new business opportunity—whether it's a new piece of business or a new job. Getting leads, referrals, and introductions that evolve through this hierarchy of ongoing exchanges of support throughout your circles is your ultimate goal. The reason I created these Five Levels of Exchange was to help people realize that you can't think of *closing* deals before you effectively *open up* your relationships through a dynamic *exchange* with the right people."

Lance nodded, taking copious notes on his laptop. Meredith finally finished typing her own notes into her iPad. Dan waited patiently, busying himself by closing up his pad and folding the stand that came with it. When Lance looked up, Dan had his equipment bundled and ready to go, waiting by the door.

"Are we done for the day?" Lance asked. His watch told him only half an hour had passed while Dan had been teaching them the Five Levels of Exchange.

"Not quite." Dan shook his head. "I'm done, but your work is just beginning."

Lance laughed heartily, but Dan wasn't known for his jokes. "So what are we supposed to do?" he asked.

"For the next half hour," Dan began, handing them their usual one-page guides for their current session, "I want you two to practice these levels with one another. Walk through all five levels and see how your exchange plays out. Next week, we can revisit how it went and, hopefully, keep putting these relationship-building skills to good use!"

· · · · · ·

Lance and Meredith found themselves once again at their local coffee shop office away from their offices. Meredith was sipping away at her chai tea latte with soy as she began the exchange, "So, Lance, I know you think I am so much better at this anti-non-networking process than you are, but to tell you the truth, I am very shy. In fact, when I was a little girl, I was known as 'the shy middle sister.'"

"Really?" exclaimed Lance. "It's hard to believe. Everyone I know thinks of you as the most outgoing, assertive leader in your field!"

"Well, I am a good actress," Meredith said with a sigh. "You don't realize I am shy because you don't see me every day. If you did, you would see that I spend most nights recuperating from my busy days. Haven't you ever wondered why you don't see me much between conferences or my speaking engagements? I need that downtime to recover. Anyway, what I know is that this type of one-to-one exchanging with a limited number of key, qualified people is so much better for my personality type than entering most conferences or networking events and having to work the room."

"Really, Meredith? Wow...well I'll tell you, learning this new insight about you gives me a little comfort—I'm not as much alone in this process, so to speak!" Lance smiled. "Okay, so let's try Level 1: The Social Exchange. Would your shyness story count as a good beginning?"

"Absolutely! In fact, telling it to you now, I suddenly see why I should integrate that into my authentic story."

"I agree." Lance nodded. "You had me hooked from the beginning. Good emotional connectivity."

"Well, it is authentic," Meredith stated soberly. For the first time ever, her smile revealed a veil of pain underneath it. Lance reached out and grabbed her hand.

"Now I understand what makes you tick even more and why you love to help and mentor others," he replied reassuringly. "Now, let's move on to the next level of exchange—Level 2: Information Exchange."

"Yes, let's!" Meredith bounced back to the present with her usual perkiness. "For the Information Exchange, let me offer you a site I just discovered today. It's called 'InMaps' and it's offered by LinkedIn. It offers you the opportunity to visualize the clusters of contacts in your network graphically and zoom in and out to see the trends—for example, who the 'bridgers' are in your network—linking you to groups of connections."

"Great! I love the sound of that! Have you heard of the new tool CardMunch? It's also a LinkedIn app. It allows you to take a photograph of someone's business card after meeting at some business function. From there, you can send a request to link to them on LinkedIn. It helps with keeping track of turning contacts into connections that matter."

"We're on a roll!" Meredith clapped her hands together enthusiastically. Then she leaned in, took a deep breath, and continued, "Okay, now for Level 3: Knowledge Exchange. I would share that my experience with social media is showing me the best thing we can do to keep up with this fast-paced social world is to choose just one online place where we do most of our connecting. For me, it's LinkedIn—the business Facebook."

Lance nodded before contributing, "Ah, well for me, it's LinkedIn, but even more so the group I just started. One of the guys in my office asked me to start a finance group for restaurant owners. I was surprised to see that within the first couple of weeks, I have more than a hundred people who have asked to join."

"Really? Maybe I should consider a group."

"Well, why don't I look at areas that aren't represented yet on LinkedIn that might turn into an opportunity for a group that addresses an unmet need? I would be happy to share my insights and offer suggestions."

"Deal!"

"Great. Moving right along, Level 4: Connection Exchange."

"Hmm, I've been thinking about this," Lance reflected. "Ever since we started working with Dan, I've been thinking about Karen, our social media director, and you. Originally, I thought it would be a waste of time to connect you two because we aren't looking for any help in our media strategy. But now I realize that you two just need to know each other. Karen is passionate about what she does and shares your philosophy of work. I think you guys need to connect."

"That's great," Meredith said, with a knowing tone in her voice.

"Indeed," remarked Lance. "It could also lead to a Level 5 Exchange: the Opportunity Exchange. Here, I realized today when I was looking at my second-degree connections on LinkedIn that there is someone I want to meet that you have within your network, Meredith. It's actually your colleague James's brother who works over at McConbrey Brothers Restaurants—one of the biggest high-end restaurant chains in the country. I would like to meet him to see if our accounting firm might be of support in helping them with a second opinion on their tax returns this year. We have found that by offering prospects a second opinion on their last year's tax returns, we have often been able to identify some pretty significant tax savings."

"Well I think they would at least want to hear your story and consider a second opinion," said Meredith. "I'll see what I can do." She paused while Lance took a moment to sit up straighter, smiling more broadly than she had seen him smile in a long time. Evidently, he was hitting his stride. She continued, "Finally, for me, I see that someone just connected with me with whom you have a third-degree LinkedIn connection."

Meredith paused for a moment while she pulled the information off of her LinkedIn app on her iPhone. "It's a woman named Debbie Scher. She's the CMO of a company I've been trying to get into for two years. It looks like your direct report, Sarah Abrams, is connected to her."

Lance was busily writing down Meredith's request. "Okay, got it. I'll go back and see what I can find out. Looks like we've got a bit of work to do, but all in all, wow! It's a lot easier having this structure in place."

"Yes." Meredith smiled. "It's also strange we have not done this before. It's like that proverb, 'the shoemaker's children go barefoot,' which is about how we often neglect taking care of those closest to us. Let's do it differently from here on out. And now that we actually have things stirring in our respective pipelines, 'let's make hay while the sun shines,' which is another good proverb!"

With that, the two of them stopped for a moment before packing up their things to look once again at the guides Dan had handed them at the beginning of their meeting. They both wanted to make sure they memorized each exchange level.

DAN'S SIXTH-LESSON TIPS

✓ Practice the Five Levels of Exchange, first with someone you know.

✓ With Level 1, focus on creating some kind of emotional connection. This happens when you take the time to figure out what matters most to your exchange partner. Make it personal for yourself.

✓ In Level 2, focus on information sharing, where you offer relevant data that would be of value to someone with whom you want to build further rapport.

✓ With Level 3, share your personal experiences (knowledge) and key insights regarding those experiences (wisdom) with those in your network.

✓ Level 4 advances your exchanges to an even more powerful level when you start to make connections that matter. Here, you discern which targeted connections could make a difference in your network circle partners' lives.

✓ Level 5 is where the action happens—where you make warm introductions and/or referrals. Here, you are creating opportunities that can lead to recurring exchanges of opportunities for you and as many others in your network as possible.

LEARN TO MAKE GREAT INTRODUCTIONS

MEREDITH AND LANCE were already seated comfortably in the hotel conference room when Dan came bouncing through the door. He looked more dressed up than usual, his dress slacks crisper somehow, and his white shirt more fitted, his tie a real eye-popper.

His smile was beaming as he shut the door behind him and stood in front of the two chairs where Meredith and Lance had plopped themselves, looking harried but buoyed by the previous week's assignment.

"Hi," he bellowed, two tones deeper than his usual voice. He then shoved his hand in Meredith's direction. "My name's Dan and I'm here to help you!"

He shook her hand energetically, then turned to Lance and repeated the procedure. Lance and Meredith shared a conspiratorial look as Lance covertly twirled his index finger around his temple in the universal sign for *somebody's going cuckoo* while Dan was taking his usual seat.

"Now," Dan said, sighing heavily as he loosened his tie and unbuttoned his top button, "why do you think I bounded in here today, acting like a crazy man?"

"Uh," Lance offered, looking at Meredith uncertainly, "you wanted to show us what we probably look like when we were networking?"

The three shared a good laugh. "Almost," Dan confessed, wagging a playful finger, "but not quite."

Dan turned to Meredith and seemed to be waiting for a response. Almost on instinct, she guessed, "Well, perhaps today's lesson has something to do with...making a good impression?"

Dan nodded, sliding the laptop bag off his shoulder. "Yes and juxtaposing that good first impression with good *introductions*. Further, I'll share with you how introductions have become the new referral."

"Interesting!" said Meredith slowly.

"I don't get it," Lance retorted, shifting in his chair and shaking his head side to side.

"Don't worry, Lance. I'll bring you along by showing you what I am talking about," responded Dan with a gleam in his eye.

There was a small coffee table between their three oversized chairs, and Dan quickly booted up his notebook computer, plugged his power cord into an outlet in the floor, and started jamming away at his keyboard.

His new MacBook Air was sleek with a large screen, and he smiled when the program he selected opened. With his smiling face bathed in the bluish-whitish light from his screen, Dan explained, "Today, I am going to make formal introductions for each of you to two trusted people in my Primary Circle.

"What's really exciting," he continued, "is that these connections will be tailor-made for you, and I'm going to make the introduction literally right before your very eyes."

As he was speaking, Dan pulled a pad of sticky notes from his computer bag, wrote a name down on the top one, then handed it to Lance. On the second sheet, he wrote down a name and then peeled the note off, handing it to Meredith.

She read it immediately; it said, "Lee Seymour."

Meredith wasn't sure whether to be excited or disappointed. Dan continued, "What we're doing now, what *I'm* doing for you two today, at this point in our relationship, is helping you build better relationships from the start. So, yes, it's only one name for now, but trust me, it's for your own good."

Meredith itched to ask a question that was on her mind, but Lance beat her to it. "Not to sound ungrateful," he said to Dan, "but...why just *one* connection?"

"For now, it's the only thing to do," Dan explained patiently. By the look on his face, Meredith was certain that actually wasn't enough for Lance.

"And here's why, Lance," continued Dan. "A good relationship builder doesn't overwhelm his partners with too many connections. One good connection, one strong connection that has been carefully screened and just as carefully targeted, is going to be more than enough if you handle it right. Remember *quality* over *quantity* when it comes to building your Primary Circle? Well, the same holds true for building *out* when you first get started in this process of making connections that matter. When I came in today, I started out in my first connection with you showing you how many people start connecting with others. They probably don't intend it, but they are way too pushy. I came on like that to help you experience the powerful difference there is between introducing yourself and having someone known and respected by someone you want to meet introduce you effectively. I am going to show you what great introductions look like."

He paused, adjusted his computer screen and projector, and then pushed a button on a remote control that automatically pulled down a projection screen in the back of the room. With a few more adjustments, he had the screen on his notebook computer transposed onto the wall at the back of the room, making it much easier to see.

"So what I'm doing now," he explained, logging onto LinkedIn, "is showing you the profiles of the people I'm connecting you with. Meredith, let's start with you."

Meredith inched forward in her seat unconsciously, even though the screen was more than big enough to provide her with a crystal-clear view of what Dan was doing. She watched as his virtual mouse pointer clicked on Lee Seymour's LinkedIn profile.

Meredith quickly scanned Lee's online profile. She was the CEO of a local chain of nurseries called Lee's Trees & More. Meredith instinctively smiled. She drove by one on her way home every day. It was odd to put the pieces together as Dan scrolled through her online profile, even as she pictured the busy nursery at an even busier intersection.

Lee sold much more than trees: she ran a busy landscaping business and sold personally customized Adirondack chairs right by the side of the road, with old-fashioned, hand-lettered price tags. Some of the chairs looked like hot dogs, some like hot rods, all were charming and many was the time Meredith had sat at a red light, staring at one, tempted to put on her blinker, pull in, and buy one for her back garden.

"Meredith," Dan was saying, "you'll see how I targeted Lee specifically for you for a variety of reasons. Look at her profile, the charities she's involved with, her list of connections. She's as passionate about what she does as you are, but she's clearly reluctant to go electronic. I spoke with her last week and all her marketing is hard copy, real-time. None of it's virtual or digital. Meredith, I think you could certainly help realize her vision in a way that aligns with the brick-and-mortar world she's created for herself—and quite successfully at that."

When Dan paused, Meredith asked, "You said she was reluctant, Dan. How reluctant?"

He smirked, opening a new e-mail on the giant screen in the back of the room. "Did I say reluctant?" He chuckled. "More like...agnostic. But you'll see, you two have a lot in common. Now I want you to see how I'm doing this from inside the LinkedIn system. This way I can attach your profile, Meredith, as well as a few select references."

Meredith watched as Dan handpicked two of Meredith's 45-plus LinkedIn references. Then he quietly began composing his LinkedIn letter of introduction. "The qualities that I think will resonate most with you, Lee," Dan typed in the e-mail field as Meredith and Lance watched, "are her top two strengths—being a good listener and being great at building strong, long-term relationships with top leaders. But don't let my recommendation be the only one you receive on Meredith's behalf. Here are two other recommendations that Meredith has received..."

As she watched, Dan found a reference a former client had given two months earlier: "Meredith is a joy to work with and we only wish we would have called her sooner. We would have started growing our new target markets even faster. Meredith is one of the best marketing strategists we have ever worked with because she 'gets us' and works to make sure we are 100 percent satisfied every time we hire her and her team."

Next, he found an older but similarly glowing reference from another previous client. These were attached to the original e-mail, which Dan asked Meredith to approve before he sent. "Now, Lance, let's look at your connections and find some references that showcase your top strengths and passion."

As Dan followed the same procedure for Lance as he had for her, Meredith could picture Lee Seymour opening up her letter of introduction from Dan. Not only would it be coming from a trusted source, but it would also have the power of two additional recommendations and an instant, bona fide link to Meredith's LinkedIn profile.

Talk about making a good introduction, Meredith thought to herself.

DAN'S SEVENTH-LESSON TIPS

✓ Well-done introductions translate into referrals. Don't become overly aggressive at first, looking for the winning sell or ultimate result. It's just the beginning.

✓ In today's online world, take advantage of LinkedIn— review your profile and make sure it is ready for optimal sharing and viewing by others.

✓ Ask for recommendations for current and previous positions from people in your LinkedIn connections who know you well, and offer to write one in return for them, too!

✓ When you scour your connections, you don't always have to do it with the mindset of "who can help me?" Leave some room to be able to identify how your connections could help out someone else you know. What goes around comes around.

✓ If you find yourself in need of introductions, look at your connections' circles on LinkedIn or identify a target pool of people you'd like to meet and then see what mutual connections you share.

✓ Introductions can be made in person. At live events, take advantage of the chance to learn more about others by playing matchmaker, such as Jill did when first introducing Dan to Meredith and Lance. Research the attendees or speakers who will be at the events you will be attending ahead of time. You

may even want to ask a mutual connection there to
introduce you for the sake of getting to know that
speaker or presenter!

✓ Open up a relationship by first exploring similar
interests or values
beyond business.

EXPAND YOUR CIRCLES OF CONNECTIONS

"I CAN'T BELIEVE how many times I've driven by here," Meredith said a few days later, as she was led into the inner sanctum of one of Lee's Trees & More's most popular franchises. Admiring not only the plants but the accessories, the garden gnomes, and Adirondack chairs, she gushed, "I need all of this!"

Lee pointed to a padded Adirondack chair in a back sitting area while taking the one opposite. Meredith's was shaped like a catcher's mitt and surprisingly comfortable. Lee's was shaped like a barbecue grill. Next to it was a small end table with wire legs and a mosaic tiled top. On top sat a lemonade pitcher and two glasses.

While Lee poured the pitcher into a Ball jar drinking glass, Meredith admired the older woman. She had white hair, soft and straight down to her back; she was dressed in vibrant colors that matched the outside seating area she had chosen for their meeting. There was a vibrant green awning hanging over a lush back deck. The entire back area was bursting with color from every type of flower and tree she thought she had ever seen in every garden she had ever been in.

Meredith looked over at a small desk up against the back wall. "What an amazing outdoor office!" Meredith gushed, taking her first sip of ice-cold lemonade.

"Don't I wish," Lee said with a wave of her hand that sent several sterling silver charm bracelets clinking together on her thin wrist. "I have my daily desk and a chair back at our corporate headquarters downtown," she explained, "but when I found out where you lived I thought I'd show off my little arboretum. I use it as a showplace during the off-season and a mini wedding chapel during the summer."

"It's darling." Meredith blushed.

Lee pinned her with an inquisitive glance. "I can't say I was surprised when I got Dan's e-mail," she explained, setting her lemonade aside. "Truth be told, I've been looking for a social media specialist for some time. I'm just concerned that whoever I choose needs to share at least a few common goals with me and have a bit of a passion or interest around my work."

Meredith nodded enthusiastically. "Frankly, Lee, I do what I do for people who are as serious about their business as I am...and I do love all things related to nature! Neither of us has the time to waste any, and if you're not ready, or eager, or trusting of my services, then I certainly don't want to waste any of yours."

Lee nodded appreciatively as Meredith realized that without Dan's introduction and the trust that had helped break down walls on her behalf, she would have never been able to speak so freely with Lee this way.

"One other thing, though." Lee paused and cleared her throat. "I do have a niece who has begged me to let her do an internship focused on social media, which she has been studying in college for two years now. She has her own blog and is constantly sending us e-mail links with great stories and pictures and . . ."

"Don't say another word, Lee. I would love to get your niece involved." Meredith smiled to herself. "I mentor at least six kids a year. She could be a big help working on your campaign and maybe even getting you to blog!"

"Really?"

"Really!" laughed Meredith.

Lee leaned toward Meredith with a big smile. Meredith took that as a cue to move the meeting along. "So, Lee, how ambitious do you want your social media strategy to be, I mean, no matter who eventually handles it?"

Lee nodded thoughtfully. "I see it like I see the rest of my business—slow and steady. I'm not interested in setting the Internet on fire and, frankly, I'd be concerned that I wouldn't be able to provide the level of customer service my guests appreciate if I did get too busy."

Meredith smiled. "One of the ways I approach a client's social media campaign is from the outside in. In other words, look at me. I've driven by this place hundreds of times but just couldn't get motivated enough to pull over. What would have given me that extra nudge? A blog post I'd read of yours? A free gardening pamphlet you offered online? A weekly newsletter? A gardening tip in the local *Weekly Reader*? My gut tells me that the personal approach is, really, the only approach to target the customers you really want."

Lee had visibly relaxed as Meredith spoke—a good sign!

"You can't imagine how good it makes me feel to hear you say that," Lee offered, reaching once again for her tall glass of lemonade. "So often marketing gurus, and I use that term loosely, are all about conquering the world and getting as much attention as they can. I just want to help provide a sanctuary for fellow nature enthusiasts or gardeners and bring a sense of peace to their lives—and backyards."

· · · · · ·

"It was such a revelation," Meredith gasped when, a few days later, she, Lance, and Dan met at their regular place, at their appointed time. "You had said Lee was an 'agnostic,' Dan, but she wasn't doubting me as much as my profession. Once we were able to connect on a personal level, all those walls of resistance came down. We're meeting later today to brainstorm the design of her blog."

"Lee? Blogging? I never thought I'd see the day," Dan remarked.

"She didn't either," Meredith gushed, "but once I was able to show her a few similar blogs—creative, noncommercial, helpful sites that actually open a door to creative expression through gardening and planting—she couldn't get enough!"

Lance was nodding right along and Meredith paused to take a breath and let him discuss his meeting. "So," he said, picking right up where she left off, "I couldn't agree more with what Meredith was saying. The man I met with, Mr. Francis, runs that giant waterfront restaurant on the wharf. The one with the lighthouse in the parking lot. Well, I knew you said he was targeted when you e-mailed him, Dan, but I didn't realize just how targeted. He confessed that he was considering opening a second restaurant over in Cobia County, and wanted me to run the numbers for that establishment."

Meredith and Dan both realized the importance of such a ground-floor opportunity and congratulated Lance unanimously. "What's interesting to me is that although I've done this before a few times, I've never been given carte blanche to sit there with the blueprints in hand and make actual, hard-copy decisions with the owner right there at the drafting table. I mean, we're talking about what kind of ceiling fans to use, how many fish tanks he can afford or should invest in. It's the most creativity I've been able to enjoy with a client in, oh, I don't know...years. I really appreciate it, Dan."

"We can't thank you enough," Meredith seconded.

Dan shook his head thoughtfully. "Come on, guys," he began. "Do you really think it was my introductions that made all the difference? Think carefully before you answer."

Meredith did. "What I think, Dan, is that your introduction collapsed the time it took to build trust between them and us. I think I speak for Lance when I say that we both appreciated your preview of each person, to say nothing of your introduction, and found that going in with the groundwork already laid for us made for a much more trusting exchange between us and the prospects.

"Personally, Dan, I was able to connect with Lee in a way I've never experienced before. Practicing the Five Levels of Exchange with you and Lance beforehand helped me figure out how to ask Lee for help and how to offer her my support."

Meredith took a rare breath, looking to Lance for support. His beaming smile sped her onward: "I realized that although I consider myself pretty good at making connections, and Lance and I talked about this very thing last week, for whatever reason, I hadn't been asking specifically for help with introductions like the one you made for me with Lee.

"Instead, I tend to spend more time with my connection exploring the types of people I want to meet. More specifically, I spend *a lot* of time identifying the industries they should work in—to be most beneficial to me, I mean—and the titles they should hold and even the psychographic aspects, such as 'people who love to learn' or 'people who regularly attended conferences,' etc. I found that, with Lee, I was more connected on a personal level, live and in person, and going into the meeting from a knowledge exchange basis really helped me focus on her needs. Well, I guess I should say, *our* needs."

Dan nodded appreciatively, then turned to Lance. "And Lance, how do you think this kind of targeted, specific, one-on-one introduction versus a mass e-mail, pick-a-business-card-out-of-a-fishbowl approach helped you?"

"I think this guy was loaded for bear when I walked in," Lance confessed. "By that, I mean the recommendation was so targeted, was so personal, that he was genuinely interested in seeing how we could help each other. I can't imagine what this type of consultancy can do for my business—the kind of value we can add to our portfolio by helping clients from the beginning of their business plan then all the way to after they're up and running."

Dan nodded, noting the obvious enthusiasm in Meredith and Lance's tales. "I'm really pleased to hear how well these two meetings went, particularly to hear how eager and enthusiastic and *open* you two were to using what you've learned. Working through the Five Levels of Exchange is all about practicing to develop a *state of mastery*.

"And you've seen that, really, these same Five Levels of Exchange are the main secret to any good relationship."

Dan's brow furrowed as he complained, "It's really too bad schools don't teach kids early on this very important set of skills. I predict that someday schools will incorporate these skills in their curriculum but for now, at least, people who get tools like this can use them to improve their networking success—their ability to make connections that matter!"

Dan began getting fidgety, a sure sign, Meredith knew, that the meeting was about to end. Before it could, she looked at Lance. In unison, they both asked, "What's next?"

After his usual bemused chuckle at how often Meredith and Lance thought alike, Dan answered, "Well, gang, the next step is all about practicing networking exchanges with others."

Lance chuckled. "Yeah, Dan, but what others?"

"I'm glad you asked," Dan said. From inside his ever-present computer bag, Dan pulled out two laminated sheets of paper. On them were printed a list of ideas for expanding their networks:

Places to Expand Your Circle of Connections

1. *Internet.* Use keyword searches for your industry to find thought leaders. When you get to know an influencer through his or her work, you might e-mail that person or seek them out through social media. You can send them a note supporting their ideas and begin

establishing a loose relationship. Social media especially has opened the doors to connecting with people who would be otherwise difficult to reach.

2. *Periodicals.* Search for both online and offline publications, newspapers, books, and article directories. These are great ways to find potential influencers, and many of them may have contact information within those publications.

3. *Conferences and lectures.* When you attend a conference, keynote, or lecture, do you introduce yourself to that person whenever possible? If not, you're missing a great opportunity.

One idea is to write a question related to the talk on the back of your business card and approach the speaker after the event. Talk with the speaker, sharing that you enjoyed their speech and that you wrote down a question you'd like to discuss for a few minutes at some point in the next several weeks. Follow up and keep any discussion to the short time you promised. This shows your respect of that person's time and can set the stage for future exchanges.

4. *Volunteering.* Volunteering pays off in connections when it's done from the heart. When you volunteer for a group or organization that you strongly believe in, a few things will happen. One, you're likely to support that group or organization for the long term, allowing you to create better connections. Two, when you do meet an influencer and establish a connection at a volunteer level doing something you both love, that connection will be even stronger and more meaningful to the influencer. Some of the best opportunities in business and life come from connections based on personal interests.

5. *Program committees*. Join an industry association and get actively involved in the program committee. This is a great place to connect with influencers in your industry on a regular basis as you book them for events. You will also create continual value for the group with quality programming and have further qualified access to group members.

6. *Alumni groups*. Alumni groups on LinkedIn especially offer a great place to build social capital with people who attended your alma mater.

7. *Traveling*. Use airline travel to its fullest! A lot of great conversations can be struck up at 35,000 feet. However, just be careful to respect your seatmate's desire to be left alone.

8. *Leisure activities*. People sometimes mistakenly believe that they can only meet influencers in work-related situations. On the contrary, in many cases great connections are made in social settings where people tend to feel comfortable sharing more. Extending yourself socially gives others a more complete picture of who you really are. For example, let's say you are the guy or girl who plays in a band and is in sales. You become much more memorable. As with volunteering, some of the best connections are made when personal interests are shared. Not all of these people are influencers, but they can become friends, which adds balance to your network. And you never know when these friends can connect you with others of influence.

9. *Current Connections*. With LinkedIn now growing by one million weekly, your network grows exponentially in the same amount of time. On LinkedIn, your connections may keep their networks hidden. Sometimes, what it takes is an in-depth conversation with a current connection to be granted access to their hidden connections. Again, it will be the way you approach and handle the exchange that will determine your success in getting introductions to your network's first- and second-degree connections.

Dan also left them with another sheet of tips.

DAN'S EIGHTH-LESSON TIPS

✓ Be open-minded and adventurous when you expand your connections. That guy on the treadmill next to you could be your new friend—and possibly a future partner.

✓ Take advantage of social media. Many users of social media share a mutual interest—they are there to meet new people and connect. They realize not every single "follower" or "friend" will be the gateway to a business opportunity, and that's perfectly fine. They appreciate the various levels of exchange. Actually, the more you engage, the more you will eventually attract like-minded people.

✓ Ask for help with introductions. It's okay—as long as you keep practicing the Five Levels of Exchange!

✓ Listen and think about how you can help someone you are connecting to before you make a request for yourself.

LESSON 9

MAKE YOUR PROGRESS AND COMMITMENT VISIBLE TO OTHERS

L ANCE SAT IN THE LOBBY of Frozen Food Stuffs, the massive restaurant chain supplier whose corporate offices were just outside town. He was dressed casually in pleated slacks and his crispest white dress shirt, working in a new pair of loafers he'd bought online.

He recognized the face of Erin Zack as she approached him in a crisp suit of ironed linen. A pale green blouse beneath the snug jacket set off her eyes. He'd seen her face, of course, on many magazine covers in recent months. After all, although she was just in her early thirties, she was already considered by many to be a thought leader in the hospitality industry, and Lance had been following many of those thoughts for months, never guessing her office was located less than an hour's drive from his own.

"Thanks for offering to meet me on such short notice, Erin," he said, standing and offering a hand.

"Glad to, Lance," she replied in a voice that sounded as young and exuberant as a college sophomore's. "I have to say, it's not every day I get such an interactive, richly detailed, and fully researched introduction. I didn't know I'd been in half those articles, let alone that anybody had read them all."

Lance tried, and failed, not to gush. "Oh, I love your premise that frozen foods don't have to taste frozen, and your stance on 'rubber chicken' is really refreshing. I also tout the production model used here at Frozen Food Stuffs."

Erin sat across from him in the spacious, sunlit, atrium-style lobby of the sprawling corporate offices and smirked. "It's funny you should mention that, Lance. I was speaking with someone in management over at Papa's Pasta Parlor and they mentioned they'd heard about us from your company, of all places."

Lance blushed and confessed, "Like I said, when I spot a new trend, game changer, or thought leader, I like to pass it along."

Erin studied him carefully. "I'm sure you understand that's pretty rare in our industry, Lance. Pretty rare in any industry, from my point of view."

Lance shrugged. "I believe the best way to get valuable information, knowledge, and especially wisdom is to exchange it, Erin, don't you?"

He could hardly believe his ears. He was sounding just like Dan. Erin smiled, toying with a lock of her curly auburn hair. "That's my philosophy anyway, Lance. I just wish more of our colleagues shared it. Do folks at your office share your value of sharing and collaboration? If they did, I can't imagine how much more effective it would be to work in that environment."

Lance looked for a moment into Erin's bright, probing green eyes. Was she asking him if there was a potential job opening at his company or was she just one of those rare, great "connectors" Dan seemed so good at finding? Lance decided that she was the latter and responded, "In my office, lately at least, I've been practicing Dan's process and found that the more explicit I am about *how* I connect with others, the better the results I achieve."

Erin looked puzzled. Lance paused a moment, thinking, and then continued. "For example, the other day I helped a colleague figure out how to go online and promote an e-book our marketing department had recently created for our potential and current clients. I had learned a couple of new Google+ and Twitter marketing strategies from someone over in our IT department who has been moonlighting as a social media marketing coordinator for a local restaurant chain. I shared my newfound online marketing ideas and they were well received. Then by tweeting and sharing just a couple of well-chosen tweets, our e-book was downloaded more than 200 times in less than half a day! Now, our whole office is tweeting and sharing updates on LinkedIn and Facebook and we're getting calls now that are a result of that free e-book being passed around the Web. Our prospects are coming to us rather than us always having to seek them out. And best of all, sharing with my colleagues has resulted in a number of other ideas about sharing our expertise on the net, such as the creation of an industry-focused group on LinkedIn and a series of monthly webinars we are all contributing to—even a possible radio show on Blog Talk Radio!"

"Wow! That sounds viral all right!" said Erin, choking back a laugh.

"Yes. What Dan helped me realize is that the shoemaker's children shouldn't go shoeless."

"Huh?"

Lance continued, "In other words, I start my networking right where I am planted currently—in my own office and within my own company. The process of making connections that matter begins right where we each work every day. This realization has helped me learn and grow and learn and grow again, to build a network that is sustainable." Lance paused again, realizing that his usual shyness, especially with people he did not know or did not know well, was nowhere to be found at the moment. In fact, he felt comfortable speaking with Erin. She was just sitting there nodding her head throughout the several minutes it took to tell his story.

Lance was momentarily distracted by the clicking of heels growing louder and louder. He looked up to find a male receptionist leaning down toward them. "Can I get you and your guest anything, Ms. Zack?"

"Lance?"

He asked for bottled water and she nodded. "Make that two, Jeffrey, and thanks."

Erin turned back to Lance. "Wow! That was a wonderful story! It puts a context around the building of networks I never thought about much before. It really makes me want to go back and start connecting with certain people in my company to see what *we* can make happen for each other and, of course, for our whole company!"

"Yes," said Lance with a nod. "Not one of us is better than two or more of us working toward a common goal that we all can benefit from. Dan also helped me realize that I am not only my own brand in this interconnected world, but I also represent, now more than ever, my whole company's brand. Further, anyone in the company who is on the Web now does the same thing. Talk about reputation management!"

"True," added Erin. "It's more important therefore that each of us becomes 'awake in the network,' if you will."

The two paused for a moment lost in their own thoughts of the implications of their conversation. Erin finally spoke up quietly, "Lance, I'm curious, how did you find such direct contact information for me?"

Her tone implied that she was, in fact, curious rather than dubious. He blushed a little and confessed, "Well, like I said, Erin, I keep a close eye on thought leaders in our industry. I set up a Google Alert featuring your name, and one day last week it alerted me to a string of tweets you were making about a new article you had been interviewed for in *Hospitality Monthly*. You posted an excerpt on your blog, so after I read that I read through some older posts, and you had mentioned taking a day off to attend the local Brewer's Fest here in Smithfield. I figured if you were that local, we must share a few connections and I found a few on LinkedIn. After that, it was merely a matter of getting past the gatekeepers in your office!"

Erin laughed breezily as they both accepted the bottled waters Jeffrey brought for them. "You know," she admitted, "I don't often read, let alone respond to, unsolicited e-mails but yours was so targeted. I never realized there was a company and experts like you and the many others in your company who exist solely to help restaurants, fast-food chains, hotels, and others in the hospitality industry do their paperwork. You offer such a niche service and I did some checking, too, and, really, you guys are one of the only companies doing what you do in my area and I like to deal with people locally. It's much more satisfying to me."

Lance gave her some background. "It's because we met through a local industry conference we attend twice a year. We are a group of introverted guys who found one another because of the fact that we are all shy. We realized after about a decade of going to conferences together, spending hours talking about our industry's leading challenges, even well into most nights while our colleagues were at bars socializing, that we had built quite a brain trust of talent. The least shy of our group, Sam Warner, came up with the idea of forming our own company. He asked us to consider the idea and give him time to present a business plan. When he returned to the next conference with an amazing plan, we unanimously agreed to unite and harvest the many opportunities none of us could create on our own. Now, five years later, we have almost 100 employees and growing. I myself started as a junior bookkeeper for Pattie's Patties, a small fast-food chain with only six restaurants. After that, I was head accountant for the Tijuana Flats Mexican franchise, when Sam presented the concept of joining Hospitality, Inc."

Erin was nodding her head enthusiastically by the time he had wrapped up his mini-memoir. "Mine was about connections too," she explained. "I started with the frozen foods division of Choc-o-Loco Ice Cream before being recruited for R&D for the Fro-Go-Yo chain of frozen yogurt stands. A few years after that, my old boss from Choc-o-Loco, who had moved to this company, contacted me and asked if I wanted to join him, and I started in the food truck division."

Lance and Erin discussed the pros and cons of their jobs for a few more minutes, until she began looking at her watch. Taking the hint, Lance stood and said, "Well, I've taken up enough of your time."

"Hardly," she said, remaining seated. "I'm just waiting for Mr. Broderick to come. He's head of our finance committee, and is interested in talking to you about how Hospitality, Inc., works . . ."

· · · · · ·

"So I have to ask," Dan began later that week after Lance had finished sharing the tale of his latest Exchanger connection, "did you get the account?"

"Signed, sealed, and delivered." Lance smiled, feeling a supportive squeeze from Meredith on his left forearm. "And I couldn't have done it without you, Dan."

Dan shrugged and waved a hand dismissively. "Not at all," he said confidently. "I really think you two are underestimating yourselves here. You had skills for opening up relationships to close deals *before* I met you. Yes, some were weaker than others and not prioritized to give you the best edge out in this new, networked world. But you both have been embracing the beliefs I have shared about making connections that matter and have leveraged those beliefs with both my connections and yours to *re-create your network*."

He paused and turned to Meredith. "Between Lance and his new account and you landing the Lee's Trees social media campaign, Meredith, it looks like you two will be busy for the foreseeable future."

"Yes, but...that's a good problem to have, right, Dan?" Lance asked.

"For sure," he hemmed, "but it's still a problem."

"How so?" Lance heard Meredith ask as he reached for his notebook; he sensed a lesson wasn't too far in the offing.

"Well, guys, let me ask you—how about your current Primary Circle? New business is always good but not at the expense of your current Primary Circle partners."

Meredith shook her head. "Between this new account and a few of the other new connections you set me up with, Dan, I confess I haven't been keeping up with my Primary Circle as often I should be."

"Me either," Lance said. "But mine isn't as big as Meredith's."

They all chuckled. "Be that as it may, Lance," Dan explained, "whoever's in your Primary Circle is there for a reason. Think how hard we worked on whittling that list down, working on the pros and cons of who should be on it. We don't want all that work to go to waste, do we?"

Lance felt it was a rhetorical question but shook his head anyway.

Dan continued. "Today, I want you both to take just a moment and think about what your Primary Circle partners have given to you so far."

Meredith nodded. "You're right, Dan. Monica introduced me to her colleague just the other day, and

Francis set up a meeting with his publicist next week. And I haven't had time to thank either of them yet."

Lance agreed. "I've got two meetings coming up next week, both of them referred to me by members of my Primary Circle, and I haven't really followed up either. I guess I figured because they're in my circle, they know that."

"But how could they, Lance?" Dan asked pointedly. "The point of being an Exchanger is to exchange constantly, now and later, not just to grab what you can and run, assuming the other person knows how grateful you are. Let them know it!"

"But how?" Lance asked.

"You should make a point of taking time monthly, or at the very least every other month, to go back and thank those who have helped you in your network. It's just as important to let them know the results of the connections they set up for you as well. Just like companies that find that 20 to 30 percent of their customers bring them 80 percent of their business, you will find the same to be true of your Primary Circle partners as well.

"You will also find that it would be much harder and take longer to build those great connections continually with new potential Primary Circle partners than to go back to your partners to see who else you know to connect them with and vice versa. In other words, it's going to be much easier to leverage your existing Primary Circle than create a new one."

"So, it's a little like a company continuing to train and nurture old employees versus hiring new ones?"

Lance asked, thinking of how his future might have been different if he'd been made to feel more welcome, even appreciated, at his earlier jobs before deciding to cofound Hospitality, Inc., with his colleagues.

"Exactly!" Dan said. "Most so-called networkers think the grass is always greener on the other side of the fence. But you and I know that watering our own lawn is the best way to achieve success. And to do that, you've got to take your Primary Circle literally. By that, I mean they are your first point of contact and should be treated as such. You should include them in the good news and the bad news. That's how great relationships are formed."

"But won't we be bugging them?" Meredith asked. "I mean, even though they're Exchangers, will they want to know every little detail of our connections? I'm not sure I would."

"No, of course not," Dan agreed. "But don't you like to hear when something you've done, some effort you've made, pays off? If you don't check back in with these people, it's the same as if they've given you a gift or thrown you a party and you never sent a thank-you card. They might not need to know the good news right away, but after a few weeks they'll start to wonder, 'How did that meeting I set up for Meredith go?' That's the time to tell them. Feedback loops are important!

"The problem with many of us is that we *assume* they already know or are too busy to care or even already understand how much we appreciate them. Remember, by making your connection activities more explicit than implicit, especially around the process I've shared with you, it helps those strong partners become even more successful with their results and new opportunities.

"One of the ways you keep others engaged with you is to keep them informed about how what they gave you has made a difference in your life and share, specifically, the outcomes of their efforts. These feedback loops go a long way to build trust and further opportunities for exchanges. Having a conversation that creates great energy and then 'goes dark' for a month is a recipe for losing momentum and credibility. Therefore, I suggest you organize and manage your relationships so that you follow up with people when you said you would.

"But," he added, "you shouldn't feel the need literally to measure how many minutes you spend each year with each person in your Primary Circle. This is too literal, but it can definitely be helpful to have a simple calendar tool or technique to let you know when it's appropriate to drop in on your Primary Circle members with some good news or simply news.

"The most important recommendation is to invest in a database—Microsoft Outlook is fine for this, for example—that allows you to note your interactions and commitments with your network. A simple list of those in your network, along with actions and current outcomes, will allow you to see who you are supporting, and who you are neglecting."

Dan paused to let his words sink in. He saw they were busily jotting down notes to follow up on their new connections and opportunities. The conversation continued through afternoon drinks and concluded with both of them committing to follow up first thing the next morning. Dan congratulated the two of them for persistence, but more importantly, for their commitment to following up. He left them both more lively and excited than he had ever seen them in the time they had been working together. When he handed them the day's lesson tips, they immediately began reading, oblivious to the growing noise from the afternoon work crowd. They didn't even realize until a half hour later that Dan had gone home.

DAN'S NINTH-LESSON TIPS

✓ Don't neglect your Primary Circle connections. Make a point to follow up, whether they have made a significant impact on your current opportunities or not. You don't want to lose them in the long run, do you?

✓ Don't feel obligated to let them know every little detail. Share important events, good and bad, to build a relationship, but create deeper relationships by sharing more than you would with those who are not in this closer circle.

✓ Continue to explore new connections.

✓ Invest in new tools, including a customer relationship management (CRM) system, to help you manage and follow your connections, such as Nimble or Microsoft Outlook.

✓ Create personalized lists on sites like Twitter, Google+, or LinkedIn. You want to keep the intimacy of your relationship.

✓ Never forget the simple power of saying "thank you!" Your network contracts and expands, but you don't want it to dissolve.

INSPIRE OTHERS

"HAPPY ANNIVERSARY!" Meredith raised a glass as Lance walked into the private dining room of one of their favorite restaurants.

She chuckled as he looked behind him, perhaps suspecting a married couple was following him inside the private room complete with candlelight and a table set for three.

"Am I missing something?" he asked, taking a seat across the table from her and spreading a white linen napkin across his lap.

"It's been three months since we first met Dan," she explained, putting down her glass of red wine. "That makes this an anniversary dinner."

"In that case..." He smiled, reaching for the open wine bottle in the middle of the table. "Let's celebrate!"

In fact, there was much to celebrate, as both well knew. For herself, Meredith had never been more successful. The journey hadn't been without its bumps and bruises, but she was a far better businessperson—frankly, a far better person—because of it.

She watched Lance as both of them awaited the guest of honor. He seemed more confident than ever, and she certainly knew his business was booming as well. He'd gotten two promotions in the last three months, due in large part to the connections he'd made and the new business he'd brought to his company, Hospitality, Inc.

Her thoughts about Lance were interrupted by his soft clapping as he stood up to welcome Dan. Though their mentor blushed at the rare display of emotion, Meredith felt compelled to stand and cheer as well.

She was one breath away from singing "For He's a Jolly Good Fellow" when Dan shushed them good-naturedly.

They sat back down as Lance poured him some wine. "At least let us offer you a toast," Lance said.

Dan blushed but made no further objection. "Here's to Dan," Lance began. "We wouldn't be here without you. What you've taught us about the magic of human relationships has truly changed our lives."

He raised his glass as Meredith joined him, eyebrows arched. She was impressed. Three months ago, she doubted he'd have had the confidence to say anything so well—or so exuberantly!

Dan seemed overwhelmed as well. "Wow, you two," Dan said after he put his glass down. "I have to say, I'm impressed. It's like, well, it's like night and day from our first meeting."

They all chuckled, but Meredith was curious. "How so?"

Dan slid his menu away. "Well, have you ever seen a deer in headlights?" he asked with a smile. "Seriously, though, you were both so convinced you knew networking up, down, and sideways!"

Meredith shook her head playfully. "Now, that's not entirely true, Dan."

"Yeah," Lance chimed in. "If we knew everything there was to know about networking, why would we have come to you in the first place?"

"Good point, Lance." Dan nodded. "I guess what I meant to say was, you thought you knew the language of networking, the letter of the law when it came to making connections. And now, I can sense that you're making truer, more valuable connections than ever before, am I right?"

"Absolutely," said Lance. "Believe it or not, my supervisors have started calling me 'that connection guy' at work. Me? Mr. Two People in His Primary Circle?!"

"But not anymore, right, Lance?" prodded Meredith.

"My Primary Circle is overflowing now." He laughed. Then quickly he turned to Dan. "But I've kept the number low enough where I can still make personal contact once a month, just like you said."

Dan nodded appreciatively as Meredith began, "Well, I can sympathize with Lance because I've never had more connections. And before, connections were never my problem, but acting on them was. Now I would say half my time is spent making quality exchanges, which in my business...well, that *is* my business."

"Yes, Meredith, but was that your business before you came to understand the true power of connecting?"

She thought about that for a minute, tempted to say "Yes," right away. But actually, that wasn't the right answer. "I thought people were my business before, but now I know that connecting with people—sincerely exchanging with them—is the fastest path to success in our networked world."

Dan nodded with satisfaction as the waitress came into the private dining area. She introduced herself and took everyone's orders, then quietly left.

Dan seemed to take the pause as a teaching moment and sat up in his chair a little as he said, "I'd be remiss if I didn't ask both of you what the difference is in how you used to approach networking with what you know today about the power of building strong, exchanging relationships. Lance, could you start? Because I think you've gotten the most out of this mini-course?"

Lance nodded energetically as Meredith smiled, if only to herself. Three months ago, he would have been begging her with his eyes for her to go first. Now there he was, up front and center, ready to share.

"I think the first thing you taught me was to trust the process," Lance began. "By that I mean, before the trusting the process, I first asked, 'what can I get?' You taught us that we have as much to give and that in giving, we actually are receiving. But even further, you showed me how to move from giving and receiving to setting up ongoing *exchanges* that make the difference between creating a *good opportunity* to creating an *ongoing series of good opportunities*. That was a breakthrough moment for me and, I think, the reason I've had so much success.

"I also think you gave me the confidence—and Meredith helped with this, too—to embrace my expertise. I forgot that I work for Hospitality, Inc., because I love the restaurant business so much. Or more specifically, love the people who work in restaurants. They're a particular breed and once I realized that I'm a particular breed, and that we're all in this together, I was really able to flourish."

Lance's cheeks were flushed and he looked to both sides for approval before continuing: "I mean, take the frozen foods account I just closed. I would have never, not in a million years, had the confidence or even the knowledge to track down Erin and approach her about our possible connections. And look how that ended up: Hospitality, Inc., is now providing paperwork solutions for the company *and* Erin and I are coauthoring a magazine article about, of all things, 'The Power of Great Connections'!"

"Lance," Meredith gushed and hugged him. "You didn't tell me that!"

"I just found out," he said, blushing in her sudden embrace. "But that's just it. Little things like that happen every day for me now."

"Me, too," Meredith agreed once Lance turned the floor over to her. "Now I actually look forward to checking my e-mail because I know someone is going to be answering a question or offering a solution or

even asking for a solution. Now I have real connections on Facebook, Twitter, and LinkedIn, and not just
a bunch of random friends or followers. It's like there's
this new energy to the connections I make, and a true
bond between myself and the connector that I never
understood or maybe never appreciated before."

Dan nodded thoughtfully as the waitress brought
their food. They thanked her and ate quietly for a
few minutes before Lance mentioned, "You know, it's
funny, but I see in my friends a lot—I mean, *a lot*—of
the same attitudes you and I had three months ago,
Meredith."

She put down her fork and nearly squealed. "I was
just going to say that. I call myself 'Mini-Dan' now
because I'm constantly lecturing my friends and family
about the way they view making connections. I literally
stopped a man from giving me his business card the
other day and insisted he give me his LinkedIn public
profile URL instead."

They shared a good chuckle over that. Lance nodded, pushed his plate away, and said, "My friends just
don't get it. A coworker, a mom of two, told me yes-
terday that because her husband traveled, she wasn't
able to go to events where she could build her network. I made her sit down with me and look at my
LinkedIn profile and my connections. I told her that
was how I was going to spend less than an hour of my
time Wednesday night, responding to comments and
queries and requesting and giving introductions. I explained that I would consider the evening successful

even if only one person responded. She looked at me like I was crazy, until the following day when we were at the same client meeting—with one of those LinkedIn connections!"

Dan was nodding, almost clapping, as Meredith watched him wipe his lips and put his napkin over his dinner plate. He smiled as she said, "I dunno, Dan, it's like we know this secret and they just don't speak the language..."

"A secret," Dan interjected reverently. "Yep, that's exactly how I felt when I first learned how to make connections that matter. It was like I had a great big secret that made me different and, frankly, gave me an edge—not something I should share with others."

Lance and Meredith looked at each other, clearly stunned. "B-b-but, didn't you figure this out on your own?" Lance asked.

"And if it gives you such an edge," Meredith added, "why would you share all this with...*us*?"

Dan smiled and sat back a little in his leather seat. "It might surprise you to learn that once upon a time, I worked in an office like most of the rest of the world. Before I started teaching and then later recruiting, I was at a software company that seemed no different from a million others just like it 10 years ago. But this one was different, because it was run by a man named Jim Wilkins. You don't know the name, but trust me, this is one of the most powerful men I know.

"And wise, too. As much as he valued my work for his company, he could see that my real strength lay in people. He put me in human resources, then sent me out on the road to colleges, recruiting people. I never really came back. I think in a way, Jim didn't want me to come back. He was my first client, and the work I did for him early on—making connections with software designers, illustrators for their game division, buyers in the malls—kept me on my feet until I could find a second client, and a third.

"But it wasn't the freedom Jim gave me that changed my life; it was this secret process of making connections that matter that he shared with me that really revolutionized the way I approached meeting people, making friends, and forging relationships that last. When I was a teacher, working and engaging with kids and parents, I used Jim's process. I also used it when I started my tutoring and later when I was recruiting. It consistently made a big difference in my success."

Meredith was impressed by Dan's story. She had seriously thought he was the originator of the process he had taught them. What's more, she still had one question. "But you still haven't told us, Dan, why you're allowing us to learn this process if it gives you such a competitive edge?"

"I have to," he said, smiling. "My mentor, Jim, told me that the price of admission to this little mini-course I now teach was this—you have to now go out and find two people to mentor in the process of making connections that matter. In my case, once I started with my first two pay-it-two-wards, as Jim would put it, I felt elated. Then after Jim passed away, I made a promise to myself that I would carry on the good work he began."

"That's it?" Lance asked.

"That's it?" Dan reiterated. "That's a lot, Lance. And, to answer your question about competitive advantage, Meredith, I know it seems counterintuitive, but this great secret grows in value only when it is shared widely. Additionally, the pie of exchanging relationships only grows, resulting in even more opportunity for everyone connected. Just think, gang, now if I ever need anybody with expertise in the hospitality or social media worlds, I'll know just who to call."

Meredith and Lance shared another look. This was all so new, and just when she thought there could be no more surprises.

"But why us?" Lance asked, reading Meredith's mind. "How did you pick us to share this information with?"

"Just as important," Meredith added, "how did you know we'd be receptive to it?"

Dan's beaming smile was like dessert after a rich meal.

"Through my introduction to you, I learned that you were both open to learning. It turns out that truly successful people are always learning. They are honest with themselves, have a drive to be better, and can handle or thrive through the inevitable ups and downs that come with trying new things.

"I got a tip that you two were both cut from the same pattern, so I felt my time would be well invested in mentoring you. What you needed most, I found, was a dose of inspiration. That's what turned it all around for you. Once you realized how powerful your story could be, and what it might mean to others, you both got so inspired there was no stopping you."

Meredith considered Dan's words. He was right!

"That's where you come in," he concluded. "Your story, progress, and results will be inspiring to others who are stuck and, if they are open to it, you can help them turn their passions into actions."

He paused, sitting forward in his chair and pinning them with a serious expression. "So, are you up for it?"

Meredith found herself nodding without hesitation. Next to her, Lance was nodding exuberantly as well.

As they left the restaurant that night, she felt a pang of regret as she shook Dan's hand. She didn't know when she would see him again and said something about her concern. But Dan replied assuredly, "Don't worry, Meredith. I put both you and Lance into my Primary Circle. Hopefully, you did the same! But, don't forget...pay it 'two-ward!'"

As they watched him drive away, Lance turned to Meredith. "Now what?" he asked, with both a serious and amused tone in his voice. They both realized the hefty weight behind his seemingly innocuous question.

"I guess now we've got to go out and find two people like us who know nothing about networking and—"

"Correction," Lance interrupted, walking her to her car. "Two people like us *who think they know everything* about so-called networking."

They both laughed before parting ways. Lance was right. Once upon a time, Meredith had imagined she knew all there was to know about networking. Now she realized all she'd known was how to make lots of connections, hoping that some of them, with little effort, would turn into referral sources or at least lead generators.

Now, as she drove away from the restaurant that night, she thought how much her life had changed since learning the power of story and, just as important, the power of making meaningful connections and setting up the right environment for mutually beneficial, ongoing exchanges of opportunities.

Suddenly, she couldn't wait to find a willing pupil to share the most powerful lesson of all: Making Connections That Matter!

DAN'S TENTH-LESSON TIPS

✓ Keep refreshing yourself on the Five Levels of Exchange.

✓ Be conscious of who is in your Primary Circle.

✓ Keep a mental and written list of Givers, Takers, and Exchangers to ensure you are connecting with the best like-minded and like-valued people.

✓ As you set out to make connections that matter, listen and give first, share your authentic story, and you become an attractor of possibility and opportunity.

✓ Adopt the pay-it-forward attitude, whether it's in making introductions, teaching someone how to make connections that matter, writing recommendations, or exchanging information and knowledge—especially about how to build connections that matter.

✓ Don't keep this method to yourself. Inspire those who you recognize will value it and share the lessons and process.

ACKNOWLEDGMENTS

FIRST WE WOULD like to thank our great team at BenBella, run by Glenn Yeffeth, for their wonderful support on this project. It was truly a collaborative process, one that defines what publishing should be—supportive, engaging, motivating, and even challenging.

Next, we thank John Willig, our agent. John, you saw our vision and championed it all the way. You also embrace our value of partnership, helping us move seamlessly through the maze of publishers trying to make sense of this new digital world. We thank you for your faith in us, and most of all, for your constant sense of humor!

FROM MELISSA: Thanks to all those great colleagues who have supported my efforts in Networlding, primarily Jocelyn Carter Miller, who originally introduced me to Larry, and who is my coauthor on Networlding. It was invaluable for me to learn how to make connections that matter with you at both Motorola and Office Depot. I also thank the folks at CDW, specifically Lauren McCadney. My experience gained in working your national team of CDW sales professionals to build beneficial, sustainable relationships was successful because of your amazing support. Thank you also to Andres Tapia, who helped me when he was the Chief Diversity Officer at Hewitt, understand that diversity of all kinds in your network (age, gender, thought, and more) enables you to achieve greater results for the common good.

Finally, thank you to Networlders throughout the world who kept me focused on building out the model of Networlding over the past twelve years. This includes my coauthor Larry, who helped me refine, test, and develop a better model for building networks inside and outside of companies like Motorola, American Express, and many small to midsized, fast-growth companies.

FROM LARRY: A huge thanks to my coauthor Melissa—her spirit, determination, and support have always been an inspiration to me personally and professionally. To my business partners Terry Barber and Carol Chapman, thank you for helping me find my own voice and for taking this incredible journey to inspiration together.

When Melissa and I started working on the concept of intentionally creating vibrant networks, it was a fairly new area of study and practice. Thank you to all my colleagues at Motorola, American Express, and Children's Healthcare of Atlanta that supported my attempts to innovate in the areas of creating communities, leadership development, and talent management. All of the opportunities I have been fortunate to have are a direct result of the wealth of connections I have made over the years. Thank you to all the exchangers in my network that have guided me, connected me, and encouraged me. Much of what I learned was from you!

Finally, I got myself on the right career track while at Motorola and my transformation was made possible by the community of people in the business learning functions and at Motorola University. A special thanks to Leo Burke, Mary Bottie, Jim Austgen, and Bill Wiggenhorn for taking a risk on an electrical engineer with a desire to make a difference.

ABOUT THIS BOOK

Are you...

   ...hoping your next networking event will be "the one"?
   ...collecting mountains of business cards?
   ...having countless breakfasts and lunches?
   ...thinking that you give much more than you get?

Then your way of networking is...DEAD.

With social networks, teleconferencing, and webinars, you are able to meet more people in more ways than ever before. But how do you create new possibilities through connections that matter? *Networking Is Dead* offers a new approach to fundamental networking misconceptions through an entertaining and knowledge-rich business story. In it, you meet Lance and Meredith, business colleagues who both consider their networking skills mediocre at best. Lance is the shy accountant and partner of a firm that specializes in

154   ABOUT THIS BOOK

restaurants. Meredith is the founder and owner of a social media marketing firm. Both of them seek direction to build their networks more proactively. Their search leads them to Dan, a specialist in creating and building what he calls *connections that matter*.

In this compelling book, authors Melissa G. Wilson and Larry Mohl show you it's the *quality* rather than the *quantity of* connections that counts.

You will learn ten lessons to help you build an effective process that:

- Deepens existing relationships and makes meaningful new ones;
- Connects across your own company to strengthen your business;
- Finds people with similar values to embark on mutually beneficial opportunities; and
- Leverages your connections instead of being overwhelmed by them.

Networking Is Dead is an engaging story that provides a specific road map designed to help you take purposeful and productive action immediately.

Networking is Dead. Literally. Make connections that matter!

INDEX